Basic
MOSAICS

Basic
MOSAICS

All the Skills and Tools You Need to Get Started

Sherrye Landrum, editor

Martin Webb,
tile and mosaic consultant

Photographs by
Tacy Judd

STACKPOLE
BOOKS

Copyright © 2010 by Stackpole Books

Published by
STACKPOLE BOOKS
5067 Ritter Road
Mechanicsburg, PA 17055
www.stackpolebooks.com

Printed in China

10 9 8 7 6 5 4 3 2 1

First edition

Cover design by Tracy Patterson

Library of Congress Cataloging-in-Publication Data

Basic mosaics : all the skills and tools you need to get started
/ Sherrye Landrum, editor ; Martin Webb, tile and mosaic
consultant ; photographs by Tacy Judd. — 1st ed.
     p. cm.
   ISBN-13: 978-0-8117-3612-1
   ISBN-10: 0-8117-3612-1
 1. Glass craft. 2. Mosaics. I. Landrum, Sherrye. II. Webb,
Martin.

TT298.B364 2010
748.5—dc22

2009027746

Contents

Acknowledgments

My gratitude and thanks to Martin Webb for sharing his considerable talent and skill in the art of mosaics. Thanks also to Caia Webb, artist and great assistant, and to Mark Klinkenberger for sharing his enthusiasm and carpentry skills. Thanks to Sam Judd for his help demonstrating techniques for the photos. Praise and thanks go to the professional mosaic artists who shared photos of their work for inspiration: Laurel Skye, Jill Rowland, Nicole Le Fur, and Mike Huffman.

I am grateful to Tacy Judd for being so cheerful and taking so many beautiful pictures. Thanks also to Janelle Steen and Wendy Reynolds at Stackpole Books for their work on the design and layout of this book.

Introduction

Making mosaics may be one of the most light-hearted crafts one can pursue because it involves gluing, painting, and assembling a picture—all the joyful activities of childhood. Mosaics are also fun because they incorporate broken pieces of tiles, ceramics, pottery, and more into works of art.

Mosaic making is similar in nature to both stained glass making and quilting. Cutting your own glass can provide you with a wide range of colors and shapes for your mosaic tiles. Stained glass designs, which have simple, bold lines, also tend to work well for mosaics.

Quilt patterns also work well for mosaic designs because the basic unit for both is a square. Unlike in the arts of stained glass and quilting, however, the edges do not need to fit together perfectly in mosaics. Nothing, in fact, has to be exact when it comes to mosaics.

There are several levels of projects in this book. The simplest ones, like the light-switch plates, introduce you to nontoxic glues and don't require cutting tiles or grouting. Projects such as these are suitable for children under adult supervision.

Light-switch plate with molded tiles and glass beads and cross with beach glass.

We then move on to cutting and shaping tiles and laying them out in a design.

You will also practice using different adhesives to secure your tiles to your base.

One of the most important things to remember when making mosaics is that once the glue dries, you cannot move the tiles again—ever. Gluing tiles directly onto a base is called the *direct* method of making mosaics.

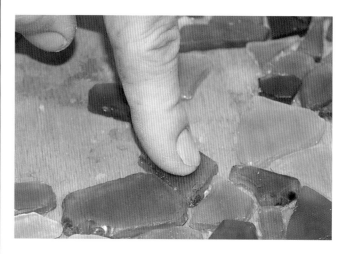

After you master the direct method, you'll learn the *indirect* (or reverse) method. This method is used when you want to create a flat surface or you need to pick up and move the mosaic to the base, such as a wall.

For the indirect method, you will cut tiles and lay them face down on transparent contact paper, which is an effective way to make a mosaic. You can see the design through the clear, sticky paper, making it easy to rearrange tiles and work out problems before you glue all the tiles in place.

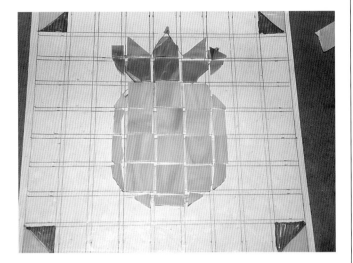

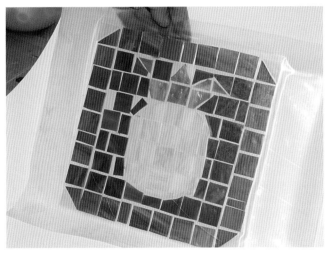

This mosaic was first laid out on contact paper, then another piece of contact paper was attached to the front of the tiles. This is called the **double-reverse** *method. Because the mosaic has sticky paper on both sides, it's easy to transport and place.*

After you've learned how to cut tiles and glue them in place, you will learn how to grout your mosaic. Although grouting is not difficult, the result can make or break the project. Each project is an experiment as well as an opportunity to create a work of art.

Modern mosaic artists on every continent are choosing new and unusual bases and adapting ancient techniques in new ways. Welcome to the world of mosaic making, where your creativity can blossom into a masterpiece.

© LAUREL SKYE

ix

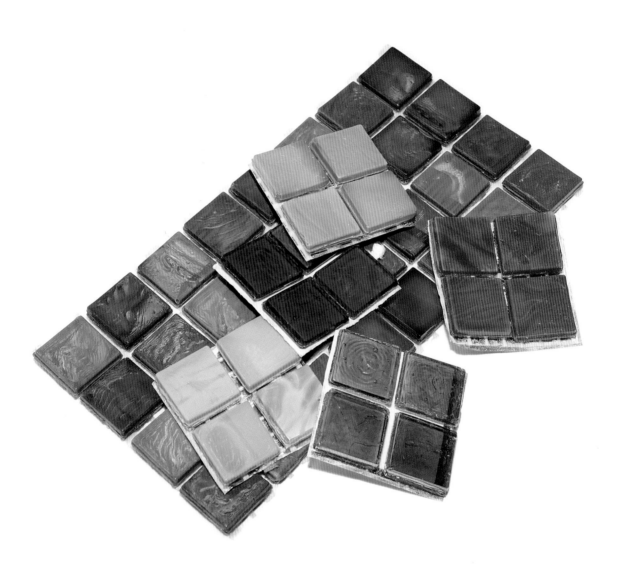

1

Tools and Materials

There really are no set rules in making mosaics except in regards to safety and choosing the right adhesive so the tiles will stick—and stay stuck. Because mosaics and tiling are in the same family, you can find most of your supplies at your local building supply store.

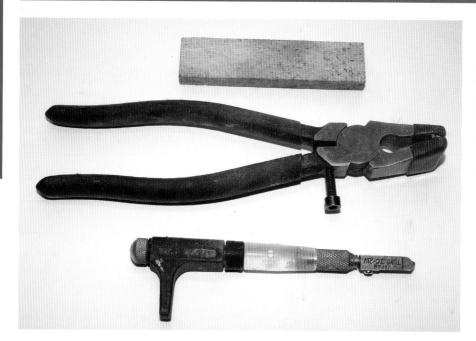

GLASS CUTTING TOOL, RUNNING PLIERS, AND CARBORUNDUM STONE
These tools cut stained glass, glass tiles, and mirror tiles. The carborundum stone helps smooth rough tile edges, but you don't need to buy one when you're first starting out.

The curved edge of the running pliers breaks the glass down and away from you.

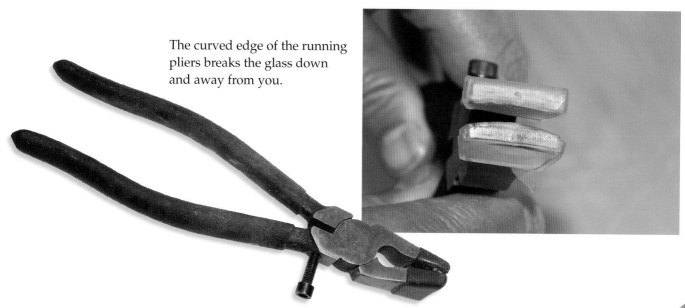

The scoring wheel of a glass cutting tool should be lubricated with household machine oil. This will keep it working smoothly when you are cutting the glass.

TILE SCORE-AND-SNAP

The tile score-and-snap tool is two tools in one. The tiny wheel on one side scores the cutting line. The "snap" side breaks the tile by pressing down on it over a raised point. This tool is used for ceramic tiles, which are thicker than glass tiles.

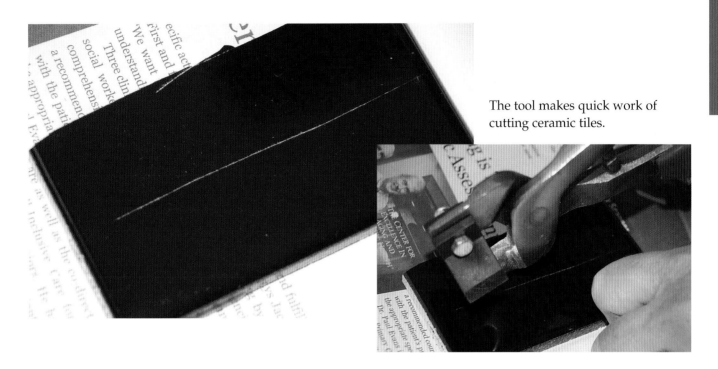

The tool makes quick work of cutting ceramic tiles.

TILE NIPPER

A tile nipper can also be used for cutting ceramic, marble, and glass pieces. You may find that the stained glass cutter with running pliers (for stained glass and molded glass tiles) and the score-and-snap tool (for ceramic tiles) provide better control when making straight cuts than the tile nipper does. The wheeled nipper on page 10 also gives you more control.

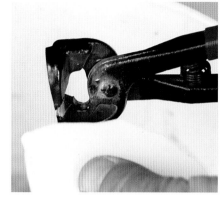

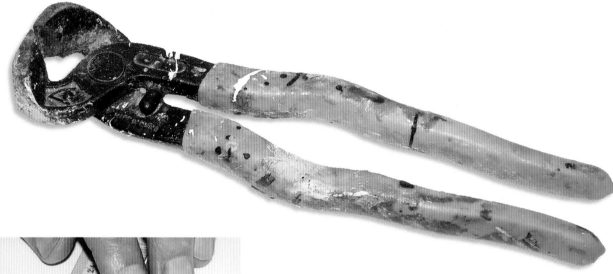

RULER

You will want to keep a ruler handy to mark straight lines before scoring and cutting your tiles.

BRUSHES

Used to butter tiles with adhesive and paint edges of finished projects.

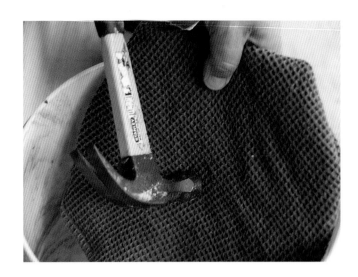

HAMMER

Used to break tiles and large pieces of crockery. (Pieces should be wrapped in a towel before smashing with the hammer to avoid injury from flying shards of china.) Also used to attach hangers to the back of projects.

PALETTE KNIVES

Used to apply adhesive and grout. Metal tools should be cleaned with water immediately after using; otherwise, any dried glue may be on them permanently. You can also use a craft stick, plastic knife, or wooden chopstick to spread the adhesive, and your gloved hands to spread the grout.

NOTCHED TROWEL

A notched trowel can be used to spread the adhesive on the base, creating deep grooves to help the tiles stick. You could also use a plastic fork to make the grooves, which should extend through the adhesive to the base.

TROWEL
Used to mix and
apply grout over
large surfaces.

**BUCKET OR
MIXING BOWL**
Used to mix and
carry large amounts
of grout.

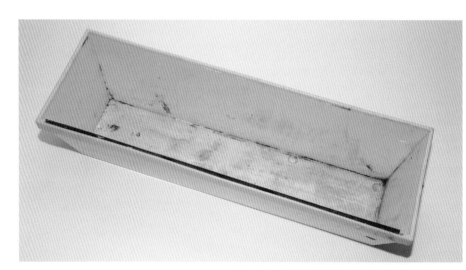

FLOAT OR SQUEEGEE
Used to spread the grout over the entire
project. For the projects in this book, you
could also use your gloved fingers or a
rubber kitchen spatula to spread the grout.

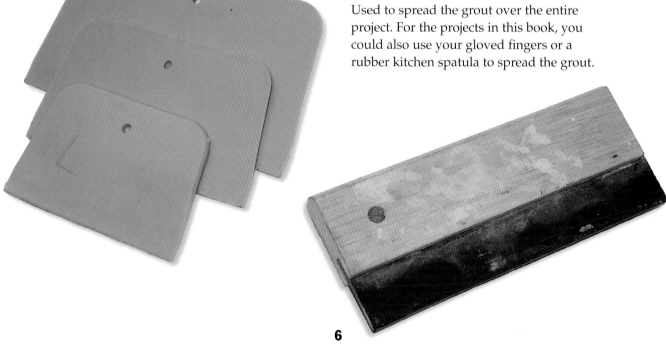

SPONGE
Used to wipe away excess grout.

TOWELS
You'll need at least two towels: one for buffing the tiles after grouting and removing excess grout, and one for wrapping the crockery to protect you from flying shards.

PLASTIC CONTAINERS OR RESEALABLE PLASTIC BAGS
Used to store tiles sorted by color.

DRAWING AND TRACING PAPER
Used to create an original design then transfer it to your project.

MARKER, WAX PENCIL, PENCIL, OR CRAYON
Used to trace the design on the base and mark cutting lines on the glass.

TRANSPARENT CONTACT PAPER

Used as a temporary base for the tiles in the indirect method of making mosaics.

MASKING TAPE

Used to protect the edges and other areas of the project from grout or paint.

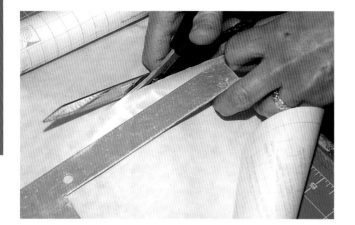

BRUSH AND DUSTPAN

Used to clean up tiny bits of glass and tile. You should also wipe the entire area with a damp sponge to remove any unseen residue. Do *not* brush shards away with your bare hands—you'll get cut.

GOGGLES OR GLASSES WITH PLASTIC LENSES

Protect your eyes when cutting tiles, glass, or crockery. Also used to protect your eyes from grout powder and cement dust.

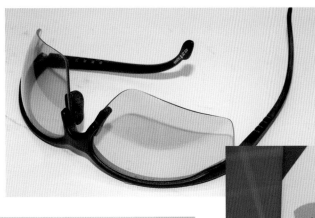

ADHESIVE BANDAGES

Be prepared for cuts by keeping bandages close at hand.

FILTER MASK

Prevents breathing fine particles into your lungs, especially when cutting glass and mixing grout. You can also wear a simple paper mask such as the kind that painters use.

LATEX GLOVES

Used to protect against cuts caused by glass or tile shards. Latex gloves allow you to feel your project better than if you were to use rubber gloves.

RUBBER GLOVES

Used to protect hands from cement and grout.

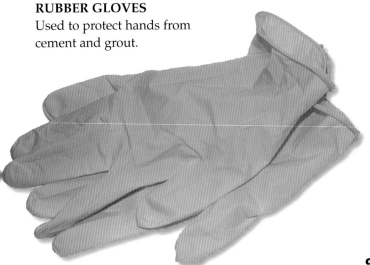

Safety Rules

1. Wear goggles or plastic glasses to protect your eyes when cutting tiles and glass or when you mix and apply grout.

2. Never brush the work surface with your hands. Wearing rubber gloves will not prevent cuts—you'll get holes in the gloves and may get cut anyway.

3. Wear gloves to protect your hands from adhesives and grout. This is especially important with epoxy, cement, and cement-based adhesives, which contain lime that can burn your skin.

4. Wear a filter mask when cutting tiles or mixing powders so you don't breathe in tiny shards of glass or dust.

5. Always use an old bucket or bowl to mix adhesives or grout. Never use a sink or bathtub because the chemicals will seep into the water system.

6. Never pour grout down the drain—it can permanently block the pipes. Let leftover grout sit for a day until the solids settle in the bottom of the bucket. Then carefully pour off the water and scoop the solids into a plastic bag and put it in the trash.

7. Clean up after every session. The tiniest glass shard can injure children or pets—or you!

Other Tools

The following tools are not necessary for the projects in this book, but you may consider investing in them in the future if you get serious about your mosaic making.

CHIPPER NIPPER
Special scissors designed to cut curved tile pieces.

NEEDLE-NOSE PLIERS
Used to handle small pieces, remove loose tiles, and replace tiles after regluing.

WHEELED NIPPER
Designed for cutting detailed shapes. This tool gives you greater control than tile nippers, but it is usually more expensive. If you decide you like making mosaics, you'll want to try this tool.

GROZING PLIERS
A common tool in stained glass making, grozing pliers are used to nibble away bits of glass and further shape a cut piece.

Tiles

Mosaic tiles are known as *tesserae* (tess-er-ay), the Roman word for squares. Tiles can be made of many things, such as glass, clay, marble, crockery, stones, shells, or jewelry.

Tip: Check to see whether the glass tiles are actually made in Italy or using the "Italian process." So-called "craft" tiles, such as those made in China, are not fired to the high temperatures of the Italian method and may crack in extremes of heat and cold such as under a hot pot or outdoors.

VITREOUS GLASS TILES

These tiles are made by pouring hot liquid glass into molds. They are a uniform shape and size, which is usually ¾-inch squares. You can also purchase vitreous glass tiles in 1-, ½-, and ⅜-inch squares.

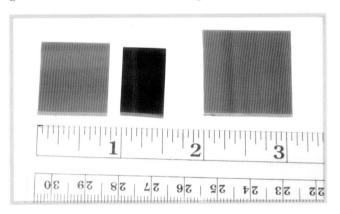

MOLDED TILES

Molded tiles are smooth on one side and grooved on the other. The grooves help the tiles grip the adhesive. Some of the projects in this book use tiles with the grooved side up because the grooves create an interesting texture that catches the light. The choice is yours.

If you buy tiles on a sheet of twenty-four, lay the sheet flat in a pan of water to soak until the tiles are released from the glue. Do not stack sheets or they will stick together. Glass tiles also come in ½- and 1-pound bags.

STAINED GLASS

Stained glass provides an amazing range of colors in translucent and opaque forms. It comes in large sheets that can be cut into smaller sections with a glass scorer.

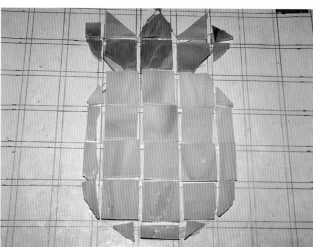

Opaque glass provides bright, shiny colors in the pineapple design.

Use translucent stained glass tiles if you're working with a clear base such as the glass candle votive.

The size of stained glass tiles will vary because they are cut by hand. Sheets of stained glass give you the option to cut larger tiles if you desire.

To store sheets of glass, wrap each one individually in several sheets of newspaper to prevent them from scratching each other. Then write the color of glass on the newspaper so you don't have to open all the packages to see which is which.

13

Another benefit of stained glass is that you can cut tiles in any size you like. The ½-by-¾-inch rectangular tiles in the background of the birdbath were specially cut to add variety and contrast to the square tiles in the starfish.

Remember that stained glass comes in various thicknesses that could cause a problem if you need to have a flat surface such as a trivet or tabletop.

Also, opaque stained glass can have different colors on each side. If you are working with the indirect method, be sure to place the color that you want face down on the contact paper.

MIRRORED GLASS

Mirrored glass is inexpensive and easy to cut, and you might be able to get free pieces from a glass cutting shop or buy precut pieces. You must use mirror glue or silicone to protect the silver on the back of the mirror. You should also spray the back of mirror tiles with clear acrylic spray to protect the silver backing.

CERAMIC TILES

Ceramic tiles are the least expensive and come glazed or unglazed. They are good for beginners to practice scoring, cutting, and shaping with the tile nippers. Glazed tiles have a hard, shiny layer of color on the surface that reflects light. Unglazed tiles are the same color throughout and do not have a shiny finish.

Often used in bathrooms and kitchens, ceramic tiles come in many sizes. Some come mounted on plastic mesh or connected with tabs of glue so you can attach them all at once.

Some ceramic tiles have a rounded edge that you can place on the edge of your project, but that edge can be tricky when you are cutting through it.

Floor tiles are thicker than wall tiles, and they're both thicker than glass tiles, which could make a difference if you want a flat surface.

Depending on their composition, some ceramic tiles will crumble into powder instead of breaking neatly. Try cutting one to see what it does before you buy a large quantity.

SMALTI

Smalti is enameled glass made in Venice. It is expensive and difficult to work with, so the beginning mosaic artist may want to start with something simpler. Smalti is fired in large slabs and cut into small rectangles. The tiles are either placed close together, no leaving room for grout, or pushed into the adhesive, forcing it up around the tiles to look like grout. (Never put grout on the surface of smalti because it will stick in the ridges and holes on the surface of the tile.)

Gold smalti is made with gold leaf layered between two sheets of glass and fired in the kiln. It is beautiful but expensive. You can have fun making your own version as described on pages 59–62.

MARBLE AND GRANITE

Marble and granite are traditional materials for mosaics. They can be bought in rods and cut with tile nippers. You can also buy them in sheets of ready-cut tiles.

CROCKERY AND CHINA

Crockery and china are an inexpensive source of mosaic materials and provide a variety of colors and textures. You can use broken dishes or buy sets of dishes at auctions and thrift shops. The technique of using broken crockery in mosaics is called "pique-assiette" (peek ah-see-et), meaning broken or stolen plate. It was named after a Frenchman in the 1930s who covered every surface of his house inside and out with mosaics made of crockery.

Tip: Check with local pottery and glass studios to see if you can have the castoffs and broken pieces from the kiln. Ask about annealed glass, which won't freeze or explode. Check with stores that sell dishes to see if they have any broken ones to give away. Glass factories that make tempered glass may also have castoffs you can have for free.

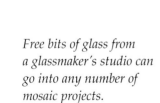

Free bits of glass from a glassmaker's studio can go into any number of mosaic projects.

Other Materials

Stones, corks, buttons, game pieces, bottle caps,
costume jewelry, shells, acorns and more . . .

© TERRY HUTSON

18

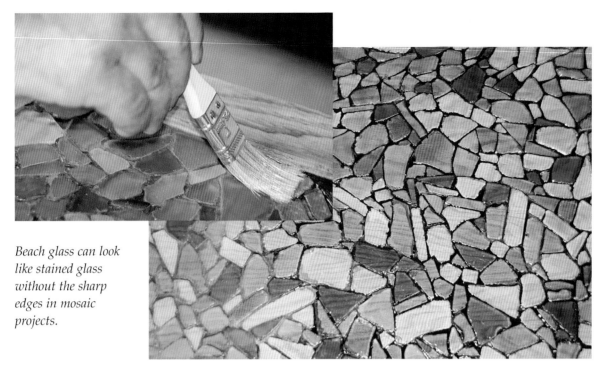

Beach glass can look like stained glass without the sharp edges in mosaic projects.

You can buy bags of glass beads, polished river stones and pebbles, and beach glass at craft stores and some home stores.

Semiprecious stones and polymer clay beads or tiles are great to work with.

19

Bases

You can glue mosaics onto almost any surface, as long as it is stable and firm. When you've honed your skills on the projects in this book, you may start planning mosaics for the top of an old table, the inset on the kitchen cabinet doors, or the backsplash over the stove.

Laurel Skye began her career by designing a mosaic on a toaster, for which she won a prize at a local bagel bakery. She has created mosaics on a guitar, French horn, cowboy hat, and this pillow—advanced projects for sure.

The key is to make sure your base is sturdy enough for the weight of the tiles and that it won't move and crack the tiles or grout. (Laurel Skye has a method for rendering the pillow firm enough to support the mosaics.)

Fiberboard or MDF

Fiberboard is good for beginners because it is inexpensive, strong, lightweight, and easy to cut with no splinters. You can have pieces cut to size at the store where you buy it or cut it yourself with a saw. (Always remember to wear a face mask while cutting.) MDF is good for small projects, but its tendency to warp makes it unsuitable for outdoor projects or large areas.

Plywood

Plywood is good for indoor projects such as tabletops. Marine plywood can be used for outdoor projects. Always seal the surfaces to prevent water from warping the board.

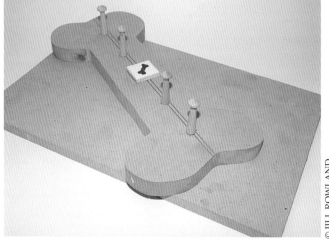

20

Linoleum Tile

Linoleum tile is inexpensive, strong, and waterproof, making it a good base for beginners. You might choose to put felt pads on the back of the finished project so it won't scratch countertops or furniture.

Wedi (Weedy) Board

A newer product that is lighter than MDF, wedi board can be easily cut with a utility knife, and it's waterproof—no sealing is necessary. Special washers are used to attach screws and hardware to the back.

Cement

Cement is a useful base for outdoor projects, such as stepping stones, birdbaths, sculptures, and step risers.

Wood

Wood makes for a strong surface, but you will need certain tools to cut it. Wood also must be sanded or sealed before you add a mosaic design.

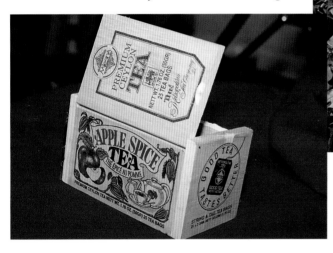

Styrofoam

Styrofoam is lightweight, inexpensive, and comes in many shapes and sizes. It forms the base of this mosaic egg.

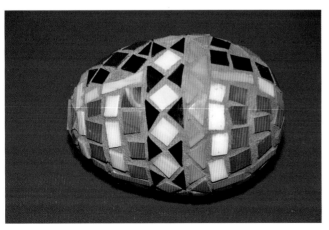

Glass and Acrylic

These transparent bases are good if you're using translucent tiles. You should use clear-drying silicone or epoxy glue for the best results; Weldbond also dries clear. If you purchase a flat piece of glass for a base, get the edges smoothed at the glass shop. Make sure the adhesive covers the entire tile so no grout gets under the tiles.

Contact Paper

Clear, sticky paper can be used with the indirect or reverse method. Don't buy shelf paper—it isn't sticky enough. You can also store cut pieces of tile between two sheets of contact paper so they won't knock against each other or get lost.

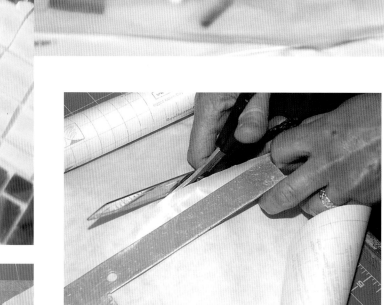

Adhesives and Glue

Glue Rules

1. If you are using silicone or epoxy glue, open the windows and doors and be sure to wear a face mask. You'll need excellent ventilation and fresh air when using these types of glue.

2. Follow the manufacturer's directions.

3. When in doubt, ask a salesperson for advice.

4. If you use too much glue, it will squeeze up around the tiles, which prevents the grout from getting into the grooves. Putting glue on the tiles instead of applying glue to the base can help you get just the right amount of glue on the tile.

5. Never let glue dry on the surface of the tiles. Wipe them clean while the glue is still wet.

6. Do not use "super" glues for mosaics.

Adhesives are used to attach the tiles to the base. It's important to make sure that the adhesive you choose will work equally well on your tiles and your base.

For indoor projects, an **all-purpose adhesive** like Weldbond will work well.

Cement-based adhesives are durable and strong, so they are best used for outdoor projects. It costs less to mix your own cement-based adhesive from powder then stir in the acrylic or latex additive to make it weatherproof. Read the directions! **Epoxy and silicone glues** are also weatherproof.

Never pour an adhesive down the sink. It will harden in the pipes and result in a very expensive plumbing bill.

Once you add adhesive, you must put the tiles on it immediately. Allowing the adhesive to dry will make the surface uneven and bumpy, and any tiles that you try to apply later will not stick well. It's very difficult to scrape off dried adhesive, so plan your design well in advance and have all your materials on hand before beginning to apply tiles to the base.

Some silicone is best applied with a caulking gun.

Silicone glue smells bad, but it dries clear, so it's best for glass-on-glass projects. It also works well for mirrors because it doesn't affect the silver backing. A tube of "liquid nails," a weatherproof silicone glue, costs about $5 and can be used to make about ninety small projects.

Epoxy 6000 comes premixed in a tube, dries clear, and is also good for glass-on-glass projects, such as vases and large candleholders. It's also useful for outdoor three-dimensional projects such as a birdbath. Months after you've finished your project, the tiles will still be holding strong and there will be no cracks in the glass.

White craft glue, such as Weldbond or carpenter's glue, is good for indoor projects. Many mosaic artists use Weldbond because it bonds almost anything to anything and dries clear. It's nontoxic and doesn't have a strong odor.

You can use children's craft glue, such as Elmer's brand or tacky glue, on many projects, but read the label to see which materials it will bond. You don't want pieces falling off your project after it's been grouted.

An epoxy was used on this outdoor candleholder.

Grout

Grout is the material that fills the spaces between the tiles and strengthens the finished project. The color of the grout will change the appearance of your project, sometimes making the colors less bright or the design less distinct. Sometimes it blends the colors so the project comes together in a whole new way.

Grout comes in a variety of colors and textures. Unsanded grout is used for indoor projects with small grout lines (approximately ⅛ inch), such as the lines between the tiles on a bathroom wall.

Sanded grout is used for wider lines between tiles (up to 1½ inches) and for outdoor projects. Most mosaic artists use sanded grout, which has a definite sandy appearance. This is fine on flower pots, stepping stones, and trivets, but the Ukrainian egg (page 117) might look better with unsanded grout.

You can also purchase premixed grout, though it's more expensive than the grout powder that you have to mix yourself. Beginners, however, may find premixed grout to be less messy and easier to use.

This birdhouse project was made with premixed grout/adhesive. Using premixed grout saves you several steps in the process, but you should first test a small area to make sure the product works and looks the way you want it to.

When you're working with beads, stones, or tiny objects that might get lost in the grout, you can either put the grout around the objects or put the grout on the base then push the objects in to the depth you want them to be. No matter what kind of grout you use, always follow the manufacturer's directions.

While you're shopping for grout, you may come across Portland cement grout powder, which is easy to apply, inexpensive, and comes sanded or unsanded. The drawback is that it takes two to three days to cure, so it must be kept damp in a plastic bag or sprayed often with water. This kind of grout powder is not for beginners.

26

Work Area

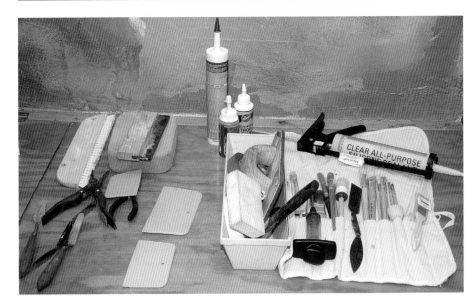

When you drop the glass votive you're working on and it shatters into a thousand pieces, you'll be glad that your workspace is easy to clean. Wherever you decide to set up, you need a large flat area with good lighting.

All your mosaic tools should be kept organized in a tool box so they are easy to locate and store.

Inexpensive plastic organizers will help keep everything handy—so will an old coffee mug.

All of your other materials should be clearly marked and stored in a safe place away from children and pets.

Cleanup is easier and more thorough if you cover work surfaces with paper you can fold up and throw away. You should clean your work station after every mosaic session no matter how short or long—all those tiny bits of glass belong in the trash.

Before beginning any mosaic project, make sure that you can work in an area with good ventilation, store your materials properly, and take the appropriate safety measures to protect yourself and others.

28

2
Basic Skills

For your first project, choose a simple design with a contrasting background so the central figure stands out. A good design has a few simple lines that define the areas you will fill in with tiles. Think of pictures in a coloring book—dark lines separate the spaces you fill with color. A color drawing can help you plan which colors to use or not use before you buy the tiles.

You can copy designs from magazines, calendars, a piece of fabric, or a rug. The idea for the pineapple design came from a bathing suit. You'll find that ideas pop up everywhere once you start looking.

As you draw or trace a picture, don't include lots of detail. Keep the design simple by drawing only the major lines. The design will evolve as you add tiles—that's part of the joy of mosaics.

You can trace a picture by holding it up to the light coming through a window.

29

Scaling a Drawing

If you have a small picture you would like to make larger, you can photocopy and enlarge it. Or you can use your ¾-inch grid and transfer the picture.

1. First draw a grid of evenly spaced lines over the picture. Use a clear ruler so you can see the picture through it.

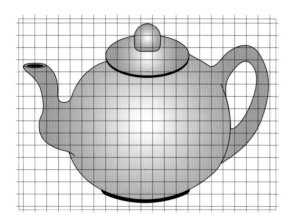

2. Look at the lines of the grid and the picture. Where do they cross? Place a dot on each grid line where it crosses a line of the picture.

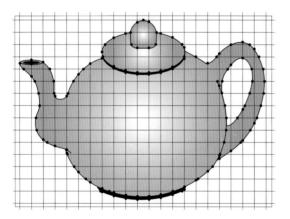

3. Transfer the dots to a larger grid, making sure to mark them at the same relative spots on the larger squares.

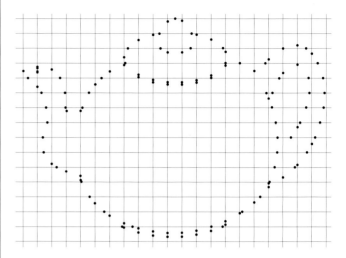

4. Now connect the dots, and you will have the outline of the picture.

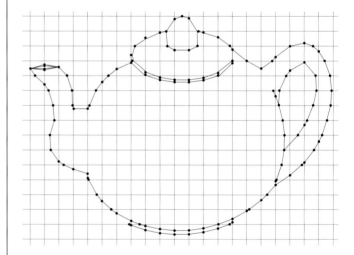

Basic Skills

© JILL ROWLAND

© NICOLE LE FUR

© NICOLE LE FUR

Borders provide a sense of order to the piece and frame the central design or subject, as shown in these examples.

Mosaic borders can also add flair to a simple picture frame or mirror.

© JILL ROWLAND

Contrasting colors, such as black and white or blue, yellow, and red, stand out against each other.

Complementary colors are close to each other in color, shade, or tone. The purple and blue are similar, but the pink tile contrasts with them.

The tiles around this mirror are complementary because the light and dark tones of blue, green, and gold all go well with the golden color of the oak.

So what colors should you use in your project? If you want the design to stand out from the background, think of street signs—white letters on red or dark green make the words pop. If you wanted the words to be difficult to read, you might have blue letters on a green background or yellow letters on a white background. There would not be enough contrast to see the words—or your design—with such color combinations.

You can use several shades of the same color to create texture and a sense of movement, as shown here.

Spots of bright color against the background make this Ukrainian egg particularly vivid.

Basic Skills

35

The three groups of tiles shown here have identically colored tiles, but each has a different color of grout. The top rows have black grout—notice how the darker-colored tiles seem to bond together? The middle rows have gray grout, resulting in all of the colors blending nicely together. The bottom rows have white grout, causing the whites and light colors to blend into the background and the dark colors to stand out individually. Such a result can split a design. When in doubt about which color of grout to use, try gray. It should provide pleasing results.

White grout makes darker colors stand out, and draws lighter colors into a solid background.

Black grout makes lighter colors stand out and draws darker colors together.

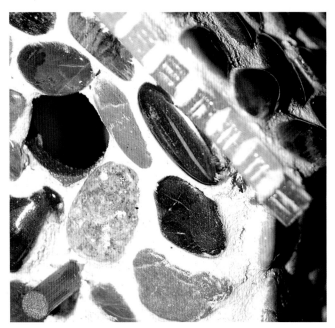

Gray grout helps blend the colors together. This is the safest choice when you're not sure which color grout to use.

You can also color your own grout by adding a dab of acrylic paint to white grout. Don't add too much or the grout will be too runny and won't harden correctly.

If you are pleased with the results, write down how much paint you used to make the colored grout so you can make it again. You may need more grout than you anticipate, or a piece might break off later and need to be regrouted.

You can experiment with the effects of many colors of grout by clicking on the "Grouterizer" tool on Mosaic Mercantile's website (www.mosaicmercantile.com).

The Distance Between the Lines

Wide white grout lines result in a fractured design. The Yin Yang mosaic shown here would stand out better if smaller tiles placed more closely together were used. Gray grout rather than white would also make a difference.

Narrower grout lines in a complementary color pull together the colors in the central design while fracturing the dark tiles on the edges.

If you are using translucent glass tiles, mirror, pebbles, or smalti, you might not use any grout.

No grout at all was used on this mosaic box that uses a wooden tea box as a base.

You can leave wide or very narrow spaces between the tiles, or you can choose to leave no space at all. If you want to make sure you leave the same space around the tiles, you can cut a ¼-inch guide from stiff paper, or use a matchstick or another item of the desired width. With practice, you'll soon be able to eyeball how closely you want the tiles to each other. Above all, strive to be consistent when placing your tiles. If you mix wide and narrow spacing, the finished project will probably look messy. Of course, if you're working with broken ceramic tiles or dishes, the distance between pieces may vary greatly.

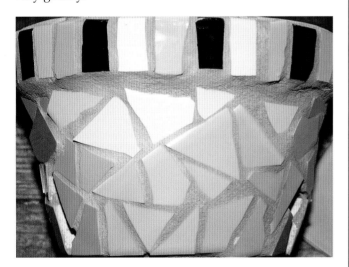

Different projects call for different treatments, but, in general, relatively consistent grout-line widths are preferred.

1. Tiles too close in color to the grout color cancel out the design. On the beige tile base, all the leaves stood out, but the light green leaves were lost in the gray grout.

2. Ceramic tiles can be stained by dark grout, so don't leave it on the tiles too long.

3. Grout may dry a lighter color than it looks when wet. If you're concerned about getting the right color, make a test patch. We made the mistake of not testing the dried grout color on the flower stepping stone. Notice how the white petals in the flower stepping stone disappeared into the grout. It was such fun shaping the flower petals and such a shame to diminish the project with the wrong color of grout.

4. Cement-based grout can be sealed after it has dried for a couple of days. Make sure the sealer you use is the kind that lets moisture from the adhesive seep out.

The stepping stone and the flowerpot were made with the same color tiles. See how the gray grout brings out the white tiles in the flowerpot?

5. Grouting objects like shells, beads, or special kinds of tiles can be tricky. Small objects can get lost in the grout, or the grout can remove the silvering on the beads or decorations on some tiles. Protect the backs of gold and hand-painted tiles with acrylic spray.

In the heart mirror project (page 98), grout was applied to the heart first, and the beads were then pushed into the grout to the desired depth.

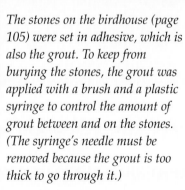

The stones on the birdhouse (page 105) were set in adhesive, which is also the grout. To keep from burying the stones, the grout was applied with a brush and a plastic syringe to control the amount of grout between and on the stones. (The syringe's needle must be removed because the grout is too thick to go through it.)

Tile, table, flowerpot, cement birdbath? The possibilities for choosing a base are nearly endless. If you choose a drinking glass or a teapot as a base, however, keep in mind that you can no longer use it to hold liquids.

If the base is dark and you want the translucent glass tiles to look bright, paint the base white.

The base of the trivet is white; the grout is sandy beige.

First you must clean the base to make sure there is no grease on it that would prevent the adhesive from sticking. Then you need to decide which adhesive will work best for both your base and your tiles.

For this beach glass cross, the glue used had to work on both glass and wood.

Be sure to read the fine print on the adhesive. Some pre-mixed adhesive-grout compounds will work with ceramic tiles but not with glass tiles.

Wood (Wood, Particleboard, MDF, and Plywood)

Always wear a mask and safety glasses when cutting wood. The surface must be roughed up with sandpaper or scratched so the adhesive and tiles will stick better. This is especially true for varnished woods, such as furniture or kitchen cabinets.

Basic Skills

Raw wood must be sealed with a half-and-half mixture of white glue (or carpenter's glue) and water.

A foam brush can be used to apply the glue-water mix to roughed-up wood, such as this wooden egg form.

Cement

If you are using a cement base, you will probably use a cement-based adhesive. Be sure to clean the base well with soap and water and let it dry thoroughly before applying the adhesive.

Metal

Before you can use any type of metal as a base, you must first remove any rust with steel wool. If the base is new, rough the surface with steel wool or sandpaper to prepare the surface for the adhesive.

Tile

Tiles usually have a glossy surface, so you may need to scuff them to help the adhesive bond, or you can use silicone or epoxy as an adhesive. If you would rather not use these adhesives, try sealing the surface with a half-and-half mixture of water and glue, then use Weldbond as the adhesive.

Glass

Your glass base must first be cleaned with glass cleaner and newspaper or lint-free cloth to remove any fingerprints or oil from your hands. Choose an adhesive that dries clear so you can see through the tiles and the base.

Terra-Cotta Pots and Saucers

If you're using a terra-cotta pot or saucer as a base, you must seal the inside and outside with a solution of half white craft glue and half water. Or you can use glossy latex paint as a sealant.

Walls

Before adding adhesive, make sure the wall is clean and dry. Then prime the surface with a good-quality primer where the mosaic will be placed. On outside walls, use a thick mixture of sand and cement with adhesive added for strength.

Three-Dimensional Bases

To determine how to place your tiles on an object, measure around the widest part (such as the top band of the votive or the middle of the egg) with a piece of paper or ribbon. Mark the circumference and put the ribbon flat on the table so you can lay out the tiles before placing them on the base.

How Much Tile Should You Buy?

Measure the area to be covered (225 tiles cover about 1 square foot). You can put nine ¾-inch squares in an 8-inch row with ⅛-inch grout lines between the tiles.

Always buy a few more tiles than you need because there will be breakage and some odd cuts that just won't fit in the project. If you are working on a larger project, order enough tiles to complete it since dye lots change. The blue tiles you bought a few months back may not match the blue tiles you buy today.

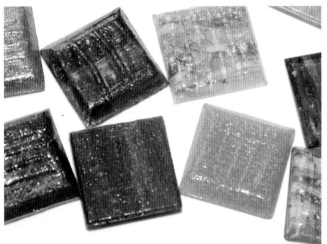

Tile colors can vary from lot to lot.

Of course there are some differences in cutting molded glass, stained glass, and ceramic tiles, the latter of which is thicker than the first two. With practice, you will get used to the differences and learn how much pressure to put on the cutting tool. When you are first starting out, the tiles might break in ways that you did not intend, which is why you should have extra tiles on hand.

Vitreous (Molded) Glass Tiles

1. Score a line on the tile.

Tip: Cut tiles away from the project to keep glass shards and dust off of it.

Basic Skills

45

2. Grasp the tile with the running pliers and align the scoring with the guide mark, keeping the guide mark facing up. Press the pliers' handles firmly together. The tile will break along the scoring. You might find that keeping the plastic coverings on the tips of the pliers will help you keep a good grip on the tile.

3. To make four smaller squares, cut the two rectangles in half. Score the two rectangles, then clip them with the running pliers.

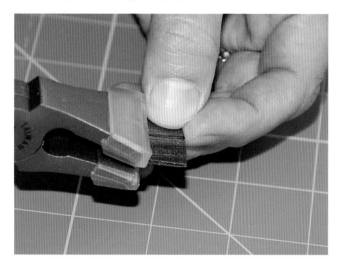

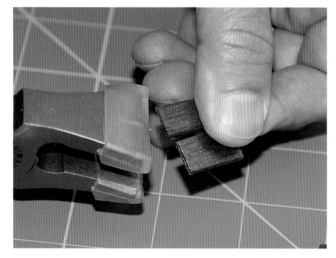

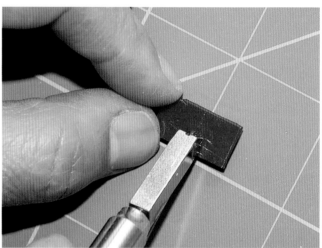

Although you can cut molded glass tiles with a tile nipper, you will probably lose half the tile. Cutting with a scorer and running pliers gives you more usable pieces from each tile.

Stained Glass Tiles

Stained glass tiles can be cut the same way as the molded glass tiles using running pliers. Make sure to cut stained glass on folded newspaper, a blotter, or even a quilter's cutting board to contain the glass shards. The quilter's cutting board is also useful when cutting straight lines.

The wheel of the scorer is lined up with the cutting line.

Tip: Opaque stained glass has a smooth side and a bumpy side. It is easier to cut on the smooth side.

Use a soft brush and dustpan to remove glass shards after each and every cut. Bits of glass on the cutting area will scratch the glass that you are cutting. *Never brush shards away with your bare hands.*

Any tools with rubber handles, such as your running pliers, can pick up little pieces of glass that could cut you when you use the tool. Take care not to leave these tools on a working area covered with glass shards.

Straight Cuts, Rectangles, and Squares

1. Use a ruler and felt-tip pen to mark your cutting lines. You can connect the dots and make a solid line to follow. The piece of glass we're cutting will be ¾ inch wide.

2. Place the wheel of the glass scorer on the edge of the glass. With one steady stroke, push down and away from you to score a line on the glass. It should sound like a zipper or a piece of paper being torn in two.

3. You can use a ruler to guide the scorer if your hand isn't steady enough to follow the line.

4. Do not go back over the line—the break will be jagged and you might damage the scoring wheel.

5. To break the glass, turn the tile over and tap along the scored line with the ball end of the cutter.

Sometimes the glass will just break along the scored line. This is easier to do with smaller pieces of glass, but tapping along the back of the scored line may help longer pieces of glass break more evenly when you use the running pliers. Tapping is recommended for beginners.

6. If the glass does not break, use running pliers to snap the glass into two pieces along the scored line. Make sure the curved blade of the pliers is on the bottom so it bends the two pieces away from you. The curved blade forces the glass to break along the scored line.

Sometimes with narrow or longer pieces of glass, the break does not go as planned.

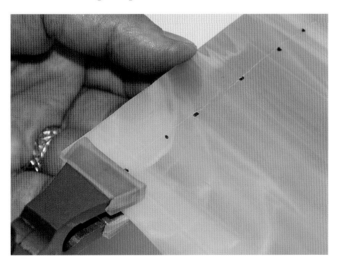

7. When this happens, move the pliers to the opposite end of the scored line and break the glass from that side.

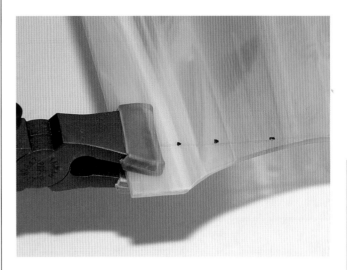

8. Clean up the jagged cut using grozing pliers or a tile nipper. Watch out for flying shards of glass. Dispose of the tiny pieces, but save any larger pieces to use later.

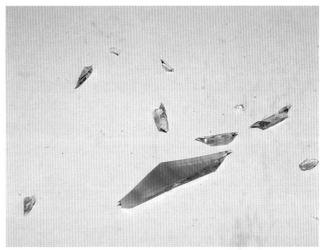

Circles

You can shape squares of stained glass into circles using tile nippers.

1. Start nibbling away at one corner.

2. Remove only a little bit of glass at a time because stained glass can shatter and send glass shards flying. It's important to have sharp blades on the nippers and hold the end of the handles to get the best leverage and cleanest cuts. You might try cutting in a box, such as a pizza delivery box, to capture the flying glass shards.

> **Tip:** When you shape pieces to fit them into a curve, trim a little off both sides of the tile, not all from one side. Cutting from one side creates too much of an angle and will throw off your design.

3. You can also cut a circle from a square using the scoring-and-tapping method, which yields fewer flying shards. Draw the circle on the glass, then draw straight lines radiating out from the circle and intersecting with one part of the curve. By cutting several straight lines, you are shaping the curved line of the circle.

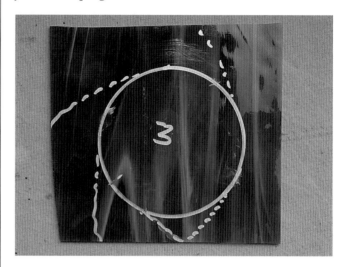

Ceramic Tiles

It is difficult to break ceramic tiles with a hammer. You will have better luck scoring large pieces and then using tile nippers to cut and shape the smaller pieces.

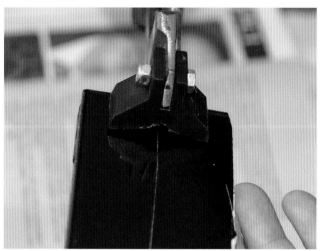

1. Cut a long piece of ceramic tile to prepare for making squares or triangles.

2. Draw the cutting line.

3. Score and snap along that line.

4. You can also cut pieces with the tile nipper. Put the teeth just over the edge of the tile and press the ends of the handles together, snapping the head of the tool upward as you cut.

These blunt-ended triangles fit into a circle.

The circle in the middle is made from a square of tile.

5. Nibble away at the corners of the tile, making sure not to cut too much at one time.

6. Hold the tile away from the nippers and nibble away the edge.

You can also shape flower petals or leaves using the tile nippers.

7. Start with a square or rectangle of tile.

8. You can nibble away freehand and see what shapes you get, or you can draw the desired shape onto the tile with a crayon (the crayon can be wiped off later).

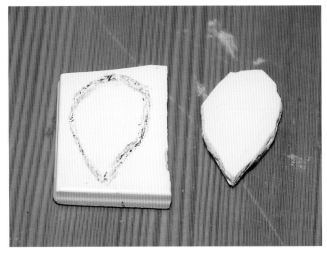

9. Start nibbling from one corner, then move to the next corner.

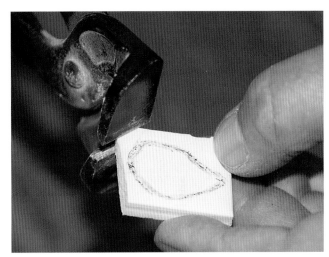

10. Keep nibbling around the entire rectangle until you have your desired shape.

Remember that slight imperfections give mosaics their charm. Don't worry if your pieces are a little jagged or uneven.

Breaking and Shaping China

1. Wrap the dish in a towel before you break it. The towel holds onto tiny shards that could cut you. Use a hammer or mallet to break the china into pieces.

Be careful of the sharp edges when you are removing the pieces from the towel.

2. If you don't wrap the dish in a towel, be sure to wear safety goggles to protect your eyes from flying pieces of glass.

3. You can trim large pieces of crockery with tile nippers. One side of the nippers is in a direct line with the handles. The other side is offset from the handles and makes a different kind of cut—more of a fine pinch.

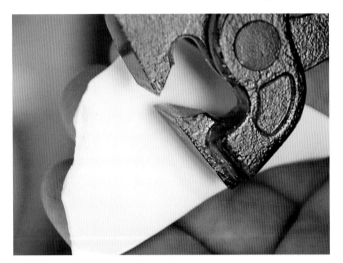

5. Use tile nippers to trim around designs you want to use or to trim and shape pieces.

4. Experiment until you get comfortable with using both sides of the nippers.

Before cutting, you can draw the shape you want on the china with a pencil if you wish.

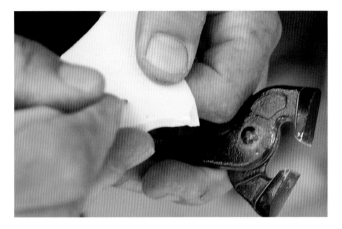

This picture frame has a mosaic border made from designs cut from the plate. As you cut the plate, lay the pieces down in order. You can then glue them onto the frame in the same pattern.

6. You must remove the ridge on the back of plates and saucers; otherwise, they will not lie flat in your mosaic.

Note the ridges on the pieces that were not used in the mosaic.

7. Remove the ridge by positioning the blades of the nippers as close to the ridge as possible, then cut the piece.

8. Carefully nibble along the ridge, taking as little of the rest of the plate as you possibly can. Odd breaks will happen, however, and that's okay.

Some types of china do not break easily, so you'll need to experiment. Microwave-safe dishes may be too hard. Some won't break unless you hit them with a hammer against a concrete floor, which is dangerous because of flying glass. Tile nippers may not work on hard dishes either. Other types of dishes will crumble into dust when you hit or try to shape them with nippers.

Gold smalti is expensive. If you would like some sparkle in your mosaic for less money, you can make your own smalti-style tiles.

Materials
Gold and silver foils
Plain, rippled, and ridged clear glass, cut into ¾-inch squares
Watercolor and acrylic paints
Iridescent paint
Paintbrush
Clear acrylic sealant spray
Weldbond glue

1. Cut plain glass tiles from pieces of glass using the glass scorer and running pliers.

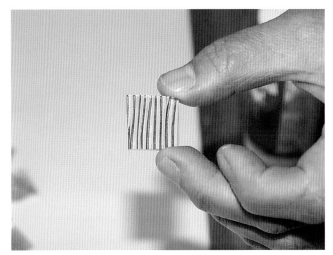

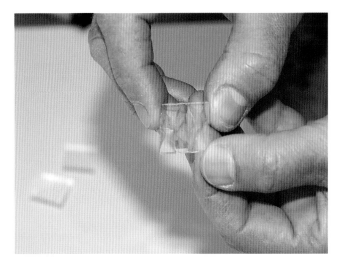

2. Remove a sheet of gold or silver foil from the package. Be careful—the foil is thin and tears easily.

Basic Skills

3. Lightly coat the entire back of the glass tile with Weldbond.

4. Place the tile, glue-side down, on a sheet of gold foil. Press down to be sure that the foil attaches to all parts of the tile.

5. Let the glue dry for 24 hours.

6. You can cut around the tiles with an X-acto knife, or you can press down on the tile and gently tear the foil away from around the outer edges. If the glue didn't cover the entire tile, you may end up with holes in the gold foil.

You can also color tiles with acrylic, watercolor, or glass paints.

Another decorating option is to paint symbols on clear tiles with gold outliner, which can be found at craft stores.

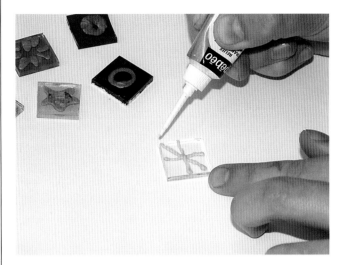

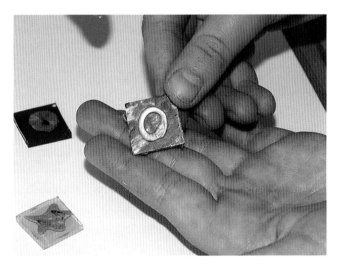

If you use gold outliner, place those tiles in a single layer in a box or somewhere they won't be disturbed. They need to dry for 24 hours before you paint the back of the tile with color. If you stack these tiles, the gold outline paint will stick to the other tiles.

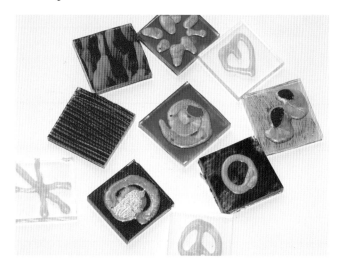

Notice that the two spirals were smudged by being stacked. The pink tile has too much gold paint and the blue one lost part of its gold spiral. The gold outline on the light pink tile to the right has picked up hot pink paint from another tile. You can still use these tiles, but next time, let them dry in a single layer.

You might choose to paint the back of each clear glass tile, or you might paint an entire sheet of glass and break off larger pieces to use in your project. Remember to let the paint dry for several hours, then seal the backs of the tiles with clear acrylic spray.

You can glue smooth glass beads to a sheet of gold or silver foil to make the shiny tiles shown here.

The foil shows through the transparent or translucent glass, creating an interesting, shimmering effect.

You can also glue the sheet of gold foil to a base, such as the wooden tea box.

When you cover the foil with clear glass tiles, the gold shines through.

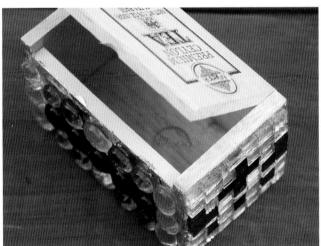

Another simple way to add shine to your project is to paint some of the stones in the mosaic with iridescent paint, which adds a touch of unexpected color and light to the surface. You can do this after the stones have been grouted.

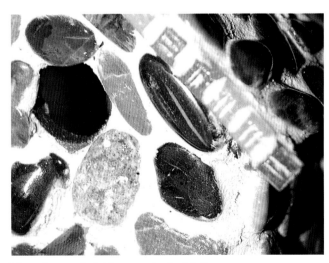

Note the purple iridescence in the birdhouse.

© JILL ROWLAND

© NICOLE LE FUR

These mosaics, by Jill Rowland and Nicole Le Fur, illustrate how mosaics can be designed to illustrate movement and flow.

The pattern you use to lay tiles into the design adds to the energy and sense of movement in the final project. This effect can be so powerful that the Romans created special names for different patterns. They called each technique or pattern an *opus*, which today is synonymous for any creative piece of work.

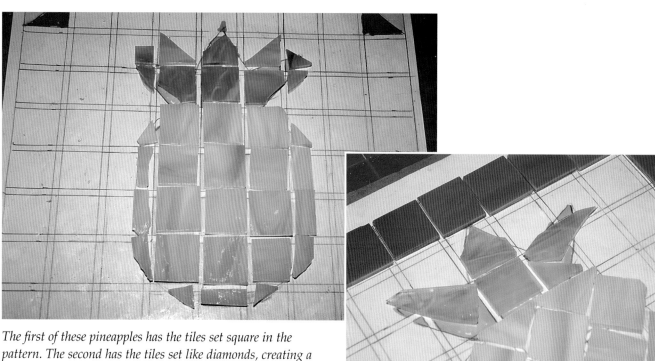

The first of these pineapples has the tiles set square in the pattern. The second has the tiles set like diamonds, creating a more natural-looking pineapple.

You can lay the background tiles in straight lines, nibbling them to fit around the central design. This technique, known as *opus regulatum*, has evenly spaced rows that provide a sense of order to the design.

Both this variation of the pineapple design and the starfish bowl feature the opus tessellatum technique.

Another method is to lay the first row or two of background tiles to curve around the central design; the rest of the background tiles are then laid in an even grid. This technique is known as *opus tessellatum.*

The tiles on the candle platter curve around the edge of the plate, radiating out from the central subject. This is called opus vermiculatum.

Another popular way to lay tiles is to make a "crazy quilt" of irregularly shaped pieces. Sometimes those pieces are mostly triangles and rectangles, which add a bit of order to a random pattern. The Romans called this technique *opus palladianum*. Mosaic artists use this method to fill in oddly shaped areas and provide a sense of movement to a design.

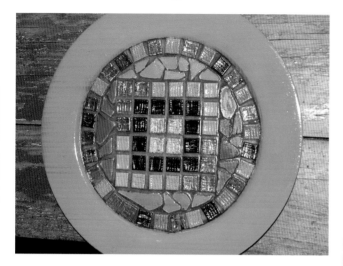

Randomly placed tiles make up most of this piece, contrasting with the regular patterning of the five large tiles.

Tip: The combined weight of the tiles, grout, and base can become quite heavy. Make sure the place you want to put your mosaic can support all this weight.

You do not have to use only one type of opus in your mosaic. For example, you might have three different patterns in one project—one for the central design, one for the border, and another for the background tiles.

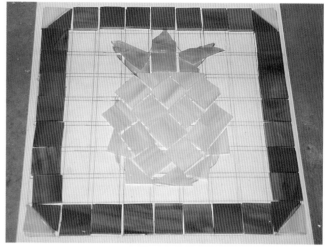

Any tiny pieces of tile should be placed last so the larger pieces can help hold them in place.

Forming the Edges

You should aim to put the rounded ends of molded tiles on the edges of the project because they are less likely to break.

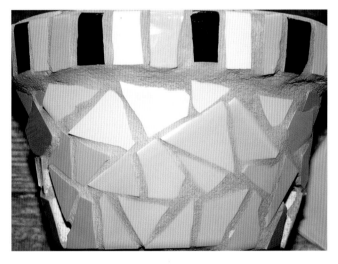

With stained glass, however, all the edges will be cut—and can cut you—so set them in a little from the edge.

Cover the edges of the project with grout to protect the tiles from getting bumped and protect you from getting cut.

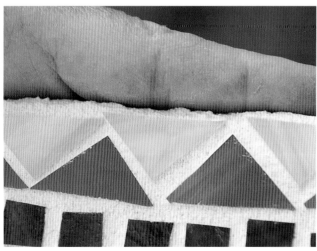

The direct method of creating a mosaic involves affixing the back sides of tiles directly to the adhesive, which is either applied to the base or to the tiles, which are then applied to the base.

1. The first step is to apply the adhesive ⅛ inch thick on the base with a notched trowel or palette knife. You can also make grooves in the adhesive with a plastic fork. The grooves are important for helping the tiles to stick.

2. Starting on the edge of the base, apply the tiles (stones in this case) to the adhesive and press them in.

3. When all the tiles are in place, let the glue dry for 24 hours.

Applying Adhesive to the Tiles

1. Instead of applying the adhesive to the base, you can apply it to the back of each tile before placing it. This is also called "buttering" the tile and is a good way to control the amount of adhesive used so that it doesn't squeeze up between the tiles, which will affect the application of the grout.

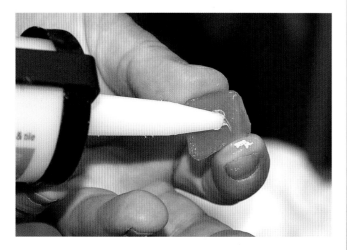

2. Press the tiles into place. The adhesive will usually allow a little "wiggle room" for you to adjust the placement if needed.

3. Needle-nose pliers can be used to place some of the smaller tiles.

4. When all the tiles are in place, let the glue dry for 24 hours.

The indirect method is also called the reverse method because you assemble the mosaic in reverse, with the back of it facing you. This method allows you to assemble a mosaic pattern then transfer it to another site.

1. To use the indirect method, cut a piece of contact paper 2 inches larger all around than the finished mosaic will be.

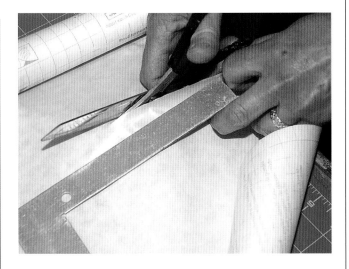

2. Remove the backing from the contact paper and tape the four corners to a board with the sticky side facing *up*. Slide the paper with the design on it underneath the contact paper.

3. Begin to place tiles on the sticky paper *with the front side down* following the lines in the design. Place the central design first, then the border, then the background.

4. Prepare the adhesive and cover the entire base with a ⅛-inch layer.

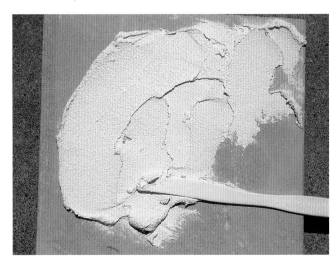

5. Use a notched trowel or plastic fork to make grooves in the adhesive.

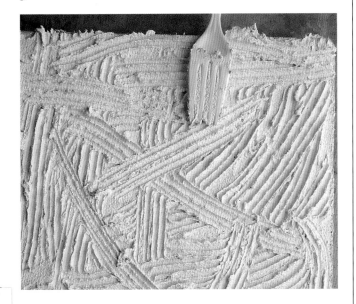

6. Pick up the mosaic and push the tiles into the adhesive, taking care to match the corners and adjust the position before the glue dries.

With molded tiles, you can choose to use either the smooth or the grooved face.

With stained glass, you must decide which side to use.

With ceramic tiles and crockery, the color is usually only on the front so you must place them facedown on the contact paper.

7. Let the glue dry for 24 hours.

8. Starting from the corners, remove the contact paper.

The Double-Reverse Method

If you are using ceramic or crockery and want to see the front of the tiles while you're working with them, you can use the double-reverse method.

1. Place the tiles on the sticky paper with the *front side up*, facing you.

2. When the design is complete, cover the front side with another piece of contact paper, sealing the design between the two pieces of sticky paper.

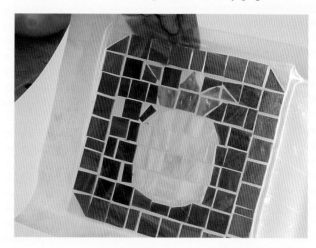

3. Then peel the back sheet away, taking care to press the tiles into position on the second sheet of sticky paper.

4. The final design is ready to be moved to the base.

If you choose to mix your grout from powder, read the manufacturer's instructions carefully. You need a bucket to mix it in, a measuring cup, a mixing tool, and water.

2. Stir the grout with a wooden stick or palette knife until it is well mixed and has the consistency of thick cake batter.

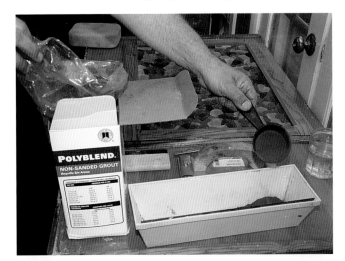

1. Measure the powder and begin to mix it with water.

3. Protect the edges of the project by covering them with masking tape.

4. Scoop or spoon the grout onto the mosaic.

5. Spread the grout into the crevices between the tiles. You can use a squeegee, a float, or an old kitchen spatula if you like.

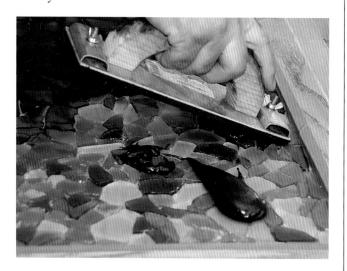

74

6. Gently work the grout into all the lines between the tiles until you have an even level across the top of the project. Sweep across the tiles horizontally, vertically, and diagonally.

7. Wait 15 to 20 minutes until the surface begins to dry.

8. Wipe off the excess grout with a damp sponge or sheet of newspaper.

9. Rinse the sponge after every swipe to avoid grinding sand into the surface of the tiles.

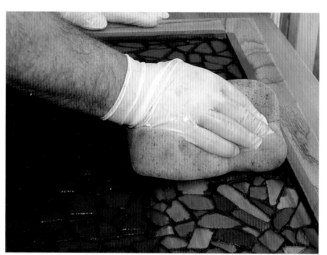

10. If the tiles are laid in a certain direction, wipe the grout off with strokes diagonal to the direction that the tiles are laid. This way you are less likely to pull up any tiles.

11. Allow the grout to dry for 30 minutes. Buff the tiles with a soft clean towel.

12. Buff the tiles again several days later. If you need to add sealer to the grout, be sure that it will let the adhesive breathe.

This beach glass tabletop was sealed with polyurethane to keep it shining and protect it from spills and stains.

13. For outdoor projects, you might use both cement-based adhesive and cement-based grout that are formulated for outdoor use. Adding an acrylic or latex mixture will strengthen these products.

14. You can mix the grout powder with acrylic instead of water to weatherproof projects, but it's best to cover the project with plastic or to bring it inside during extremely cold weather.

Cleaning Up

1. Never pour grout down the sink because it will harden in the pipes and ruin them.

2. Let the bucket you used for the grout sit undisturbed for a day.

3. Pour off the water that has separated from the solids.

4. Put the solids in a plastic bag and into the trash.

There are several different ways you can finish your project, including with tiles, paint, grout, or a wooden frame.

You should not use tiles to finish the edges of pieces that get moved around and used a lot. They will eventually break off. When applying tiles around the edges of a three-dimensional project, such as a table or flowerpot, apply the glue and let it get tacky before applying any tiles. You could also speed up the drying time with a hair dryer.

The edges of the birdhouse's roof were finished with ⅜ inch tiles.

To use tiles on the edge of your project, you must first cut the tiles to fit the depth of the base. These tiles should be at least ⅓ to ½ inch wide or they will be more difficult to handle and easier to knock off. Silicone or epoxy can be used to attach the tiles to the edge. Or you could apply white glue to both the edge and the tiles, let them sit until the glue gets tacky, and then attach the tiles.

If tiles come unstuck, you need to scrape out the grout and adhesive so that you can see the base, then reapply adhesive to the base and tile. When the glue is dry, regrout around the tile. This is why it's a good idea to keep a bit of the leftover grout in a covered glass jar, or keep the recipe if it's a special color.

Another finishing method is to paint the edges and backs of completed mosaics. Make sure you use a color that is either the same shade as the grout or that complements the colors of the tiles.

If you don't want to tile or paint the edges of your project, you can build up grout along the edges to protect the tiles from being broken and yourself from being cut. Use sandpaper to smooth any rough grout on the edges. The process is shown here.

You might also decide to protect the tiles with a wood frame cut to fit around the project, or you can set the tiles into a recessed area.

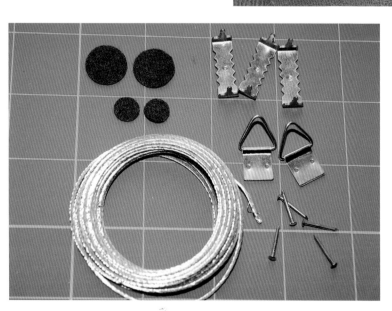

You can add hardware to hang a project on the wall, or add pads to protect your furniture. If the surface of your project is fragile, you may need to place it on a towel to hammer on the hardware. A better option would be to attach the hardware before you glue on the tiles.

© JILL ROWLAND

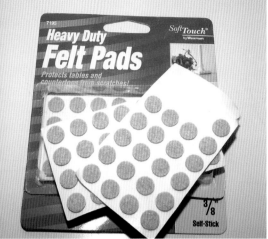

Felt circles or frame bumpers protect the wall and furniture.

If you design a mosaic around a mirror, be careful not to get glass cleaner on the mosaic.

If the tiles in your mosaic seem cloudy, try a tile cleaner from the hardware store. It's important to wipe away all the excess grout while it is still damp, then follow up 30 minutes later with a soft cloth or towel to buff the tiles.

3

Projects

PINEAPPLE TRIVET

Materials
paper
scissors
soft pencil
glass scorer and running pliers
MDF
white craft glue (Weldbond)
powdered sanded grout
gloves
sponge
bucket
acrylic paint for back of project
felt bumpers for back of project
¾-inch-square tiles
18 yellow (4 triangles)
28 orange (4 triangles)
26 blue (32 rectangles; 18 small squares; 4 small triangles)
½-inch by ¾-inch tiles
7 green (4 triangles)

This colorful trivet is a practical item to have around the kitchen.

1. The first step is to cut an 8 inch by 8 inch square out of MDF for the base.

2. Choose your colors and cut the tiles you will need for this project using an enlargement of the pattern. Sort them by color.

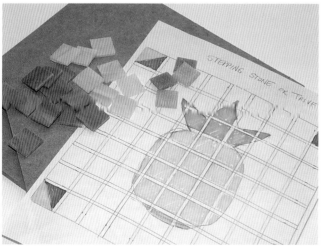

3. Seal the base with a half-and-half mixture of water and white glue, which you can brush on using an inexpensive craft brush or sponge.

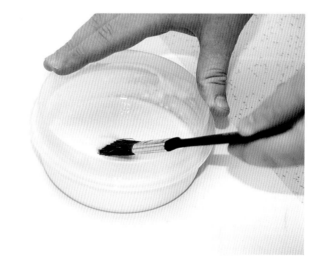

4. Trace or draw the design onto white paper.

5. The least expensive way to transfer a drawing onto a base is to use the same technique you learned in grade school. Turn the design over and, with a soft pencil laid on its side, scribble back and forth over the back of the design.

6. When you have covered the back of the paper with soft pencil lead, turn it over and tape it to the base. Trace over the lines of the design with a harder pencil or pen. (If you wish, you can buy transfer paper to insert between the paper and the base before you draw over the design.)

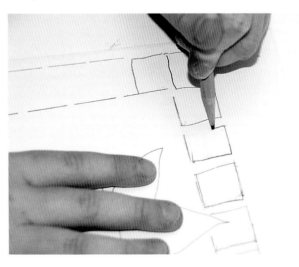

7. When you lift up the paper, you will see the design on the base. If necessary, you can trace over the lines with a felt-tip pen to see them more clearly. The grout will cover any lines you make.

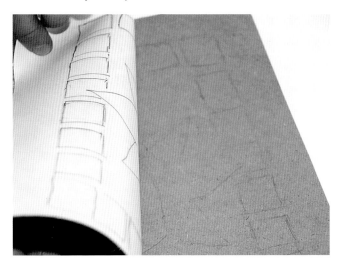

8. Now lay the tiles onto the paper design to determine if they fit and if you need to cut any more. Make any adjustments before you affix the tiles.

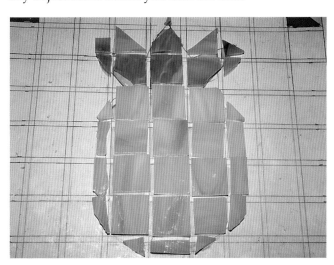

9. There are two ways to apply tiles to the base: glue on the base or glue on the tiles. You may apply glue in one area and place tiles in it, but make sure you don't let the glue dry before you have placed the tiles. You'll have about 15 minutes to adjust the position of the tiles, but once the glue dries, you won't be able to move them again.

Another option is to "butter" each tile with glue using a brush or rubber paint stick. With this method, you won't waste adhesive and you won't have to hurry to get the tiles placed before the glue dries.

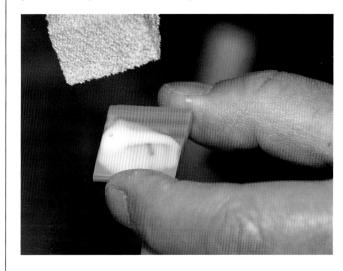

16. Spread the grout with a squeegee or another tool, taking care to fill all the holes.

17. You can protect the edges of the mosaic by shaping and smoothing the grout with a palette knife or other tool, as shown here.

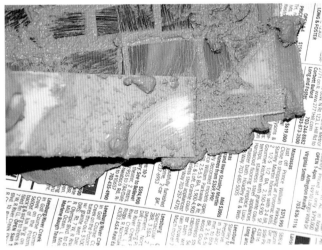

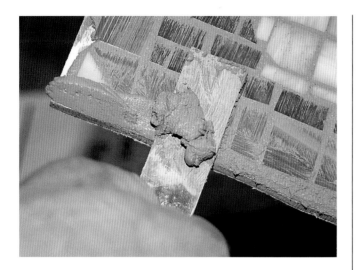

18. Let the grout sit for 15 to 20 minutes.

19. Wipe the surface with a damp sponge. Make sure the sponge isn't too wet or it will pull the grout out of the spaces.

20. Use each side of the sponge only once and then rinse it out. If you don't rinse out the sand, you'll scratch the tiles.

21. Polish any grout off the surface of the tiles with a soft cloth. Let the project sit for 24 hours so the grout can dry, then buff the tiles again with a soft cloth.

22. You may want to paint the edges of the trivet in a color that matches one of the tiles or the grout. To protect furniture and countertops from being scratched by the trivet, you can glue or apply sticky felt pads to the four corners of the underside of the trivet.

The indirect method is used to make this garden stepping stone that features a variation of the pineapple design used on the trivet. The indirect method can be used for curved surfaces, such as bird-baths, or for surfaces that need to be level, such as table-tops and floors. You can butter the backs of thinner tiles with adhesive before flipping the mosaic so they'll be the same height as all the other tiles. This will help even out the different thicknesses of the tiles.

Materials

8-inch square travertine or cement garden paver

paper

scissors

soft pencil

glass scorer and running pliers

Epoxy 6000 or Liquid Nails silicone adhesive

powdered sanded grout, cement-based for outdoors

acrylic admixture

gloves

sponge

bucket

palette knife or craft stick

¾-inch tiles

   18 yellow (4 triangles)

   28 orange (4 triangles)

   26 blue (32 rectangles; 18 small squares; 4 small triangles)

½-inch by ¾-inch tiles

   7 green (4 triangles)

1. Travertine and cement pavers can be found at home and garden centers. Wash the paver well so the adhesive will bond to it.

2. Choose your colors and, using the same design you used for the Pineapple Trivet (page 82), cut all the tiles you will need for this project.

Projects

3. A scrap piece of MDF or heavy cardboard to support the mosaic will be helpful as you place the tiles on the contact paper.

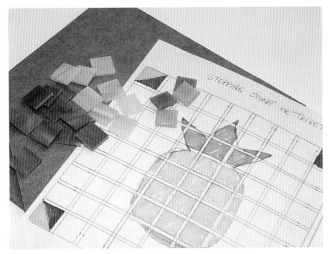

4. Cut a piece of contact paper several inches larger than the base. Remove the backing so the sticky side is facing up. Slide the paper with the design under the clear contact paper so you can see it.

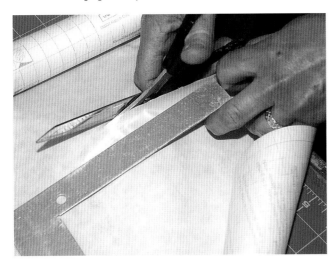

5. Tape down the four corners of the contact paper. If you don't tape the corners, the paper will stick to your fingers as you begin laying your tiles.

6. Starting with the central design, apply the tiles to the contact paper with the fronts facing down.

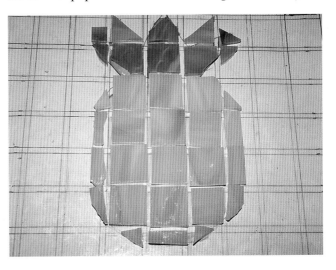

7. Then move on to laying the border.

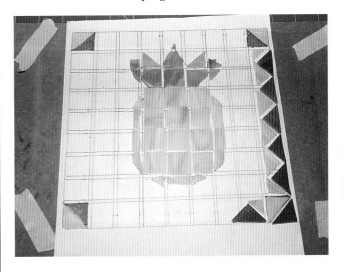

Notice that the paper design only has the four corners of the border colored in.

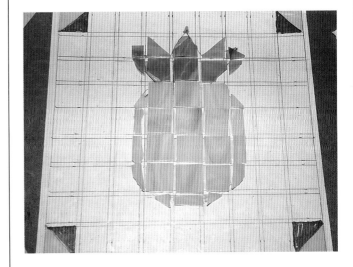

8. There are several different ways in which you can design your border. One option is to make a solid orange border with triangle corners.

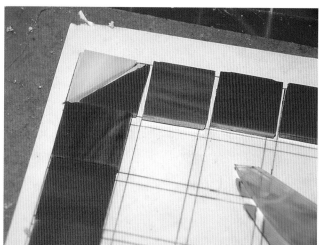

9. Another option for the border is to intersperse yellow and orange triangles along the edge. In this design, you'll still need to cut a few pieces to fit.

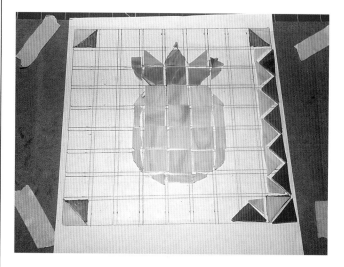

10. Once the central design and border are complete, begin laying tiles for the background. Start with the row of tiles closest to the central design and work out toward the borders.

11. Cut the final tiles to fit as necessary.

12. Apply adhesive ⅛ inch thick to the surface of the paver with a notched trowel or plastic fork. The teeth of the tool should reach down to the underlying board.

13. Carefully pick up the contact paper and turn it over to settle the tiles into the adhesive. Match the corners so the design will be even on every side.

14. When you are satisfied with the position, you can place a length of wood over the design and gently tamp it into the adhesive with a hammer. Pressure from your hands will work just as well.

15. Take care to tuck the border pieces into the adhesive and away from the edge. Let the glue dry for 24 hours.

16. After the glue has dried, slowly and carefully remove the contact paper, starting at the corners.

Go slowly so that pulling off the contact paper doesn't pull any tiles out of the adhesive, which will happen if you haven't given the glue enough time to dry.

17. If a tile comes loose, you'll need to scrape off the adhesive from the base, then reapply glue to the tile and put it in place. Let this glue dry for at least an hour before applying grout.

18. Prepare natural sanded grout for outdoor use. Mix the grout until it reaches the consistency of creamy peanut butter then drop some on the mosaic.

19. Spread the grout with a squeegee or your gloved hands, taking care to get it in all the lines and crevices.

Don't worry about covering the tiles with grout.

20. Build up the edges of the stepping stone with grout to protect the tiles on the edge.

21. Remove excess grout with a squeegee, craft stick, or your gloved hands.

22. Let the grout sit for 15 to 20 minutes until it starts to look powdery. Clean the tiles with a damp sponge. Too much water on the sponge will pull the grout out from between the tiles. Remember to rinse the sponge after every wipe.

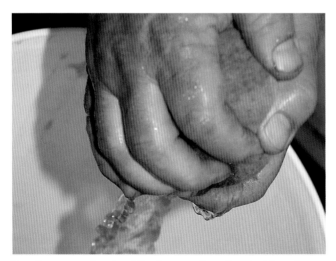

Let the grout dry for 30 minutes, then buff with a dry towel.

23. Let the grout dry overnight, then polish the tiles again with a clean, soft towel.

Outdoor mosaic projects need to be able to survive freezing weather. For this reason, you must only use bases, tiles, adhesives, and grout that are made for outdoor use. Epoxy, silicone, or cement-based adhesives and grouts are best for such projects.

Outdoor mosaics must also be sealed so that water doesn't trickle down between the tiles, freeze, and crack the mosaic. A water-seal product made for wooden decks is a suitable sealer. If the piece is precious to you, you might want to bring it into the basement or garage or cover it with a tarp over the winter.

You can sometimes use the direct and indirect methods interchangeably, whatever you wish. The only time the indirect method is required is when you need to assemble the mosaic offsite, then transport it to where it will be installed.

Materials

12 pink molded glass tiles (¾-inch)
2 glass beads
white craft glue
light-switch plate

1. Apply glue to each tile before placing it. Start with the four corner pieces first. Make sure the edges are not sticking out over the edge.

2. The tiles on each side of the switch openings are glued with the grooved side up so they are flat against the plate. This way there are no sharp edges near the switches. You can use the grooved side up on all the tiles if you like.

3. The two glass beads complement the color of the tiles and add a bit of protection to the top and bottom rows of tiles.

4. No grouting is needed for this project. If you'd like to add grout anyway, cover the holes for the switches and mounting screws with masking tape so they don't get plugged.

Tip: You can move the tiles around for about 15 minutes. The glue will have dried in about an hour but needs to sit for 24 hours to form a strong bond.

5. Mount the plate over the electrical switches using the tiny screws that come with the plate.

Projects

97

SHELLS LIGHT-SWITCH PLATE

Materials

40 small shells of various types

white craft glue

light-switch plate

1. Arrange the shells on the light-switch plate until you create a design that is pleasing to you.

2. Pick up each shell and put white glue around the outer edge, since the inside will not touch the plate. Place each shell, carefully working your way around the outside edge or border.

3. Glue and place the shells inside the border. Let the glue dry for 24 hours.

4. Mount the switch plate using the tiny screws that came in the package.

HEART MIRROR

Materials

purchased heart-framed mirror

beach glass, glass beads, and jewelry beads

white craft glue

sanded grout

acrylic paint

bucket

sponge

towel

1. Cover the mirror with masking tape or paper to protect it. Paint the inside edge, outside edge, and back of the frame with an acrylic paint that complements either your beads or grout. Let the paint dry.

2. Prepare the front of the frame by painting it with a half-and-half mixture of white glue and water.

3. Mix the grout with water. Color it with acrylic paint if necessary.

4. Use a palette knife or other small tool to spread grout on the frame until you reach the desired thickness.

5. Gently press each bead into the grout, being careful not to go too deep. After about 15 to 20 minutes, wipe away any grout on the surface of the beads. Let the grout dry for 24 hours.

BEACH GLASS CROSS

Materials

purchased wooden cross with inset area
acrylic paint (optional)
beach glass
white craft glue
beige sanded grout
palette knife
bucket
sponge
towel

1. If you don't like the natural wood color of the cross, paint the outer edges and back with acrylic paint. This cross was painted green to complement the green beach glass in the mosaic. Prepare the inset by painting it with a half-and-half mixture of white glue and water.

2. Rearrange the beach glass on the cross until you are pleased with the design.

3. Mix the grout and fill the inset of the cross with it.

4. Gently press the pieces of beach glass into the grout. If any grout gets on the surface of the glass, wipe it off with a damp sponge or paper towel.

5. Let the grout dry for 30 minutes, then buff the glass until it shines. Buff again the next day.

GREEN PLATTER

Materials

wooden platter (14-inch diameter with 10-inch inner circle)
acrylic paint (optional)
beach glass
white craft glue or silicone glue
black grout
palette knife
bucket
sponge
towel

¾-inch molded tiles for inner square

4 pearl
12 burgundy
6 light peach
6 lime green
6 dark teal

¾-inch molded tiles for outer circle

6 light teal
7 turquoise
10 dark teal
7 burgundy

1. If you don't like the natural look of the wooden platter, paint the front and back of it with acrylic paint.

2. Use a pencil and ruler to draw a line through the center of the inner circle, then another line crossing it, so you have divided the platter into four equal sections. Lay the first four tiles that make up the center square; there should be one tile in each section. Pick up each tile, butter it with adhesive, and glue it in place.

3. Next, lay the tiles for the border around the circle to see how they fit. Depending on the size of the platter, the bottom edges of the tiles may touch while the top edges are wide apart. This is a common occurrence when trying to fit squares into a curve.

4. You can apply adhesive around the circle and lay the tiles in it, or you can butter each tile with glue and place them on the base. If you apply the glue to the whole circle, you must get the tiles placed before the glue dries.

5. Return to the center square and place tiles around the outside of the center four tiles. When you are pleased with the colors and the fit, butter each tile and place it, or apply adhesive to the platter and place the tiles.

6. The next step is to place the tiles in the third layer of the square. Make sure that the corner tiles will fit between the border and the second row of squares. Glue the tiles in place.

7. Fill in the remaining areas of the platter with pieces of beach glass. If you use clear beach glass, the color of the platter will show through. You can also choose pieces that coordinate with the colors of the tiles. Beach glass fits together like a jigsaw puzzle. Once you are happy with the arrangement, glue the glass in place.

8. Let the glue dry for 24 hours.

9. Mix the grout and apply it to the platter, making sure to fill in all the lines. Remove any excess grout. Let the platter sit for 15 to 20 minutes, then wipe the grout off the tiles with a damp sponge. Rinse and wring out the sponge after every swipe to avoid scratching the tiles and glass. Dispose of the grout properly. Buff the tiles with a dry towel or newspaper.

10. Let the grout dry overnight. Polish the tiles with a soft, clean towel or cloth.

This trivet is made with molded tiles cut into a variety of shapes so you'll have the chance to practice cutting. You should cut on the smooth side of the tile, but the grooves on the back may still cause irregularly shaped pieces. That's okay. Also, when you use the running pliers, the tile may break somewhere other than along the scored line. That's fine, too. Since this is a tree, you'll want leaves of all sizes.

1. Cut all the tiles for the project.

2. Experiment with how you want the pieces to be arranged on the trivet. Keep turning them to fit until you are pleased with the arrangement. Make sure that the tree trunk only appears at the bottom, and there are glimpses of branches through the leaves. In imitation of tree paintings by Gustav Klimt, add a few gold tiles for an artistic effect.

Materials
6 x 6–inch beige ceramic wall tile
Weldbond glue or silicone
bucket
palette knife
beige sanded grout
sponge
soft cloth or paper towel
latex gloves
¾-inch tiles
10 green tiles in two to four different shades of green, cut into rectangles, triangles, and tiny squares (or autumn leaf colors of orange, yellow, and red)
5 brown tiles, cut into thin rectangles and squares to represent tree branches
3 gold tiles, cut into pieces

Tip: Because the base of this project is a wall tile, you could fit it into a wall of tiles in the bathroom or make three or four tree tiles to use as a backsplash above a sink.

3. There are two ways you could apply the adhesive. Remove one or two pieces at a time, butter them with glue, and replace them in the design. Because the tiles are small, however, this method may disturb the design too much. If you would rather glue all the pieces onto the base at the same time, you can use the double-reverse method. Arrange the tiles face up on the sticky side of a piece of contact paper cut an inch larger all around than the base. When you have finished the design, cover it with another piece of contact paper. Then flip it over and remove the back piece, pressing the tiles into the front piece.

4. Cover the base with a thin coat of glue. Pick up the mosaic on the contact paper and press the tiles into the glue. Let the glue dry for 24 hours.

5. Choose the grout color carefully. The gray grout used in this project was a poor choice because the sage green tiles of the outer leaves disappeared into the grout. Sky blue grout would be an interesting choice, as would a light tan or white grout. When you have decided, prepare the grout and grout the mosaic.

Tip: Be careful when grouting the trivet because the tiny pieces are easy to knock loose. If this happens, you need to scrape out the grout and adhesive, reglue the tile, and then regrout it once the glue's dried.

6. After 15 to 20 minutes, wipe the tile with a damp sponge. Rinse, wring out the sponge, and repeat.

Let the grout dry, then buff the tiles gently with a soft cloth. The loops of a towel could catch the edge of a tile and pull it loose.

BIRDHOUSE

Materials

wooden birdhouse

beads, stones, painted iridescent stones

white craft glue or silicone

premixed adhesive/grout

palette knife

sponge

soft cloth or paper towel

latex gloves

sandpaper

1. Sand the base with sandpaper. Apply the adhesive thickly on one side with a notched trowel or palette knife.

2. Press the stones into the adhesive.

3. Complete one area before moving on to the next. If you apply all the adhesive at once, the birdhouse will be difficult to handle, and the adhesive will dry before you have a chance to place all the stones.

4. Build up the adhesive/grout mixture around the stones. You can use a brush, plastic syringe, your gloved fingers, or damp sponge to apply the grout.

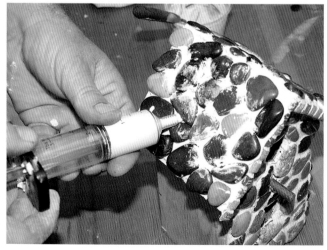

The syringe allows you to carefully control the amount of grout applied.

5. Let the grout dry for 15 to 20 minutes. With a damp sponge, carefully wipe the grout from the surface of the stones, being careful not to dislodge any stones. Uncover any stones that may have been buried by the grout.

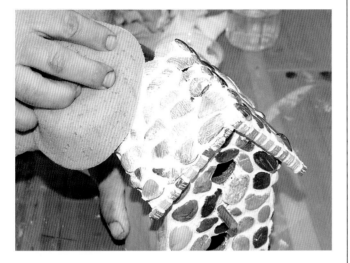

6. Let the grout dry overnight and polish the stones and tiles once more with a soft cloth.

Note: This type of adhesive/grout mixture is not for projects that will remain outdoors. Bring the birdhouse indoors when the summer is over.

1. Prepare the base by painting it with a half-and-half mixture of white glue and water.

2. Copy the design onto a piece of paper. Turn the paper over and, with the side of a pencil, make sweeping lines of graphite over the back of the paper.

3. Put the graphite side down on the base and trace over the design with a pencil or pen.

4. Lay out the tiles on the paper design. See where you will have to cut a few of the tiles to fit into the curved points, but wait to cut those pieces until after you have laid the larger tiles.

5. Starting in a corner of the border, butter each tile with adhesive and place it. Continue placing tiles around the border. Remember to allow about a ⅛-inch gap between the tiles for the grout.

Materials

8 x 8–inch MDF square

white craft glue

acrylic paint

brushes

bucket

palette or craft knife

white sanded grout

sponge

soft cloth or paper towel or newspaper

latex gloves

¾-inch molded glass tiles

   36 gold (2 shades)

   18 dark teal

   22 light teal

Glass beads

   1 gold, 1 teal

6. Glue down the two glass beads, then start laying tiles on the outer curve of the symbol. Take care to put dark tiles with the light glass bead and vice versa.

7. Cut triangles for each end of the curve, then lay the dark tiles along the inner curve. Fill in the dark area with tiles. You may need to cut a molded tile into thirds so you have three long rectangles, or you can cut smaller triangles to fit the space.

8. Next, move on to the lighter half of the symbol. Lay the tiles along the outer curve. Cut a tile into two triangles for the end pieces. Work your way around the dark glass bead and lay the tiles along the inner curve. Fill in the space with tiles cut to fit.

9. Once the central design is finished, fill in the background. Since this background is laid in straight rows, you can work from the outside in. Cut tiles into triangles to fit along the curves of the Yin-Yang symbol.

10. Allow the glue to dry overnight.

11. Prepare the grout and apply it, making sure to fill all the gaps. Remove the excess. Let it sit for 15 to 20 minutes, then wipe the tiles with a soft cloth or newspaper. After the grout has dried, polish the tiles with a soft cloth.

12. For a more finished look, paint the sides and back with acrylic paint.

Tip: If you would like greater detail in this design, cut the ¾-inch tiles into four smaller tiles. You might begin by gluing on the glass beads and making a circle of the smaller tiles around the bead. Then you can start placing tiles on the outer and inner curves of each section.

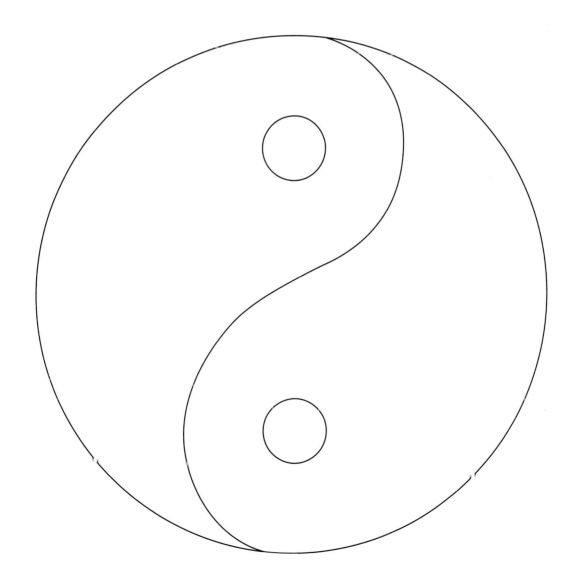

Materials

8 x 8– MDF square

white craft glue

grout

acrylic paint

brushes

bucket

palette or craft knife

sponge

soft cloth or paper towel or newspaper

latex gloves

Handmade gold and colored tiles

33 gold and painted tiles

14 shades of lime green tiles

8 mirror tiles

4 green glass beads

1. Prepare the base by painting it with a half-and-half mixture of white glue and water.

2. Copy the design onto a piece of paper.

3. Transfer the design to the base.

4. Lay out the tiles on the paper design or on the base itself. You will make a few cuts for this project, but wait to cut the smaller pieces until after you have laid the larger tiles.

5. Start with the large circle of the peace sign. Butter each tile with adhesive and place it next to the adjacent tiles, continuing on around the circle. Move the tiles closer or farther apart to get them to fit into the curve.

6. Next, lay the lime-green tiles that fit inside the peace symbol. You may have to trim the tiles at the bottom of the sign. Make sure to take a little from each side of the tile—don't cut only one side or it will be uneven.

7. Glue the four glass beads in the corners. Then, using a mirror adhesive, silicone, or Liquid Nails, glue the mirror tiles next to the beads.

8. Let the glue dry overnight.

9. Prepare and apply the grout by hand, taking care not to scratch the glass and mirror tiles.

10. Remove any excess grout. Let it sit for 15 to 20 minutes, then wipe the tiles with a soft cloth or newspaper. After the grout has dried, polish the tiles with a soft cloth.

11. For a more finished look, paint the sides and back of the project with acrylic paint.

Materials

make or purchase a framed mirror (22 x 26 inches overall with a 12 x 8–inch mirror)
white craft glue or silicone
grout
brushes
bucket
palette or craft knife
sponge
soft cloth or paper towel or newspaper
latex gloves
120 molded ¾-inch glass tiles in four or five complementary shades, such as green, blue, burgundy, and gold

1. If the wood is already finished, sandpaper it to roughen up the surface so the glue will bond. If the wood is raw, seal it with a half-and-half mixture of water and white craft glue.

2. Lay out the tiles to create a pleasing design.

3. Starting at one corner of the base, butter each tile with adhesive and place it. Don't skip around; work in a straight line to the opposite corner. Allow the glue to dry overnight.

4. Mix the grout. You need to be careful when grouting so you don't get it on the mirror or the wood. Use masking tape to protect these surfaces, then apply the grout with your gloved hands so you can keep it on the tiles only.

5. Remove any excess grout. Allow it to dry for 15 to 20 minutes, then wipe the tiles with a soft cloth. After the grout has dried overnight, polish the tiles with a soft, clean cloth.

6. Remove the masking tape. When you clean the mirror, be careful not to get glass cleaner on the tiles or grout.

Materials

- glass or ceramic plate
- red and blue ceramic tiles
- white craft glue, silicone, or epoxy
- grout
- bucket
- palette or craft knife
- sponge
- soft cloth or paper towel or newspaper
- latex gloves
- fine sand
- candle

1. Wash and dry the plate to be sure that it is clean and grease-free.

2. Use silicone or epoxy to glue ceramic to ceramic or glass. Work in an area with good ventilation and wear a face mask.

3. First lay out the inner circle of tiles to see how they fit. If you do not need to cut any tiles to fit, butter each tile with adhesive and place it on the circle.

4. When the inner circle is complete, lay the outer circle of tiles. Let the glue dry overnight.

5. Use masking tape to mark off the area of tiles where you will apply the grout. Mix and apply the grout, using your gloved hands to work it into the gaps. Remove any excess.

6. Let the grout dry for 15 to 20 minutes, then polish the tiles with a soft cloth. Allow the grout to dry overnight and polish again with a soft, clean cloth. Remove the masking tape.

7. Carefully fill the inner circle of the platter with sand to about ½ inch. Place the candle in the center.

Projects

Materials

½-inch plywood cut to desired size (the project shown here is 26 inches by 8 inches.)

3 3-inch squares of wood to back the hooks

¾-inch wood molding

mounting hardware

sandpaper

2 bags of pebbles (2 to 3 pounds each)

hammer

black silicone cork

liquid nails as needed

3 metal hooks, painted white

1. Attach the mounting hardware to the back of the project, then attach the wood squares and hooks to the front. Protect the wood around the edges and hooks with masking tape.

2. Use black silicone cork as the adhesive. Working from left to right, scatter the stones across the adhesive and arrange them to your liking. Apply slight pressure so they bond with the cork.

3. No grout is used in this project. Let the project dry for 24 hours.

Projects

Materials

4- or 5-inch Styrofoam or wooden egg

white craft glue, such as Weldbond

black grout (add black acrylic paint to white powdered grout or buy ready-mixed black grout)

bucket

sponge

towel or lint-free cloth

¾-inch stained glass and vitreous glass tiles

13 yellow, cut into 4 smaller squares

2 yellow, cut into 4 smaller squares and then cut into triangles

6 yellow, cut in half and then into thirds

9 black, cut into 4 smaller squares

9 black, cut into 4 smaller squares and then cut into triangles

7 white tiles, cut into 4 smaller squares and then halved again into rectangles

8 orange, cut into 4 smaller squares

8 orange, cut into 4 smaller squares and then cut into triangles

2 red, cut into 4 smaller squares

1 blue, cut into 4 smaller squares

Top   **Bottom**

1. Cut all the tiles as described and sort by color. The number of tiles you need will depend on the size of egg you buy. Adjust the design to fit your egg.

2. Mark a vertical and a horizontal line on the egg using a rubber band and a pencil. The horizontal line around the middle shows you where to put the first line of tiles.

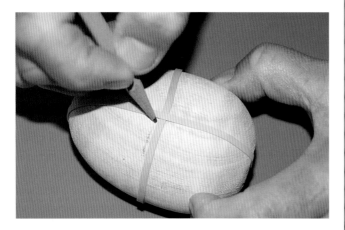

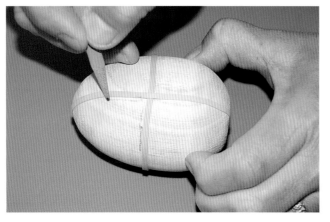

Tip

For cutting stained glass, a glass scorer and running pliers work best. Tile nippers tend to crush the glass. With the score-and-snap method, you'll get more usable pieces. Uneven pieces are okay, too. You can use them all.

Because all the surfaces of the egg are curved, you'll need small triangles that fit on the curves without sharp edges poking out. These edges could catch the towel when you are buffing off the grout and pull pieces loose. The triangles on each end of the egg are the tiniest; the triangles in the middle of the egg are larger.

There are two ways to cut triangles and get different sizes:

1. Cut the tile diagonally to make two triangles, then cut each again to make four.

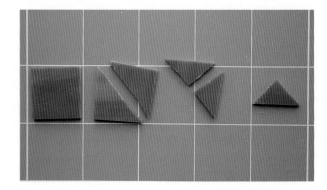

2. Cut the tile in half and then in half again to make four small squares. Cut each square diagonally to get eight smaller triangles.

3. Seal the Styrofoam or wooden egg by brushing on a half-and-half mixture of water and white craft glue. This is an important step because it will help keep the tiles from sliding off and make a stronger bond between the tiles and base.

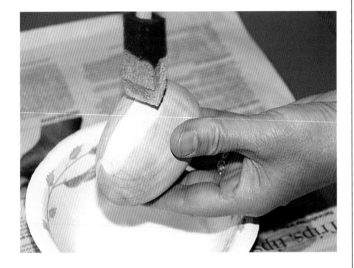

4. Butter each tile with glue, but don't use too much or the tiles will slide off. You must be patient when creating a three-dimensional project. Hold the tile in place while the glue on both the egg and the tile bond. As you continue placing tiles, check back to make sure the pieces are staying where you put them.

Tip: The side with the most tiles on it is heavier and will make the egg tip over and roll away every time you set it down. Use a folded towel to keep it in place or set it on a heavy cup so it can't roll away.

5. Start with the middle row of black triangles that wrap around the widest part of the egg. Lay the tiles so their points are up and their bases touch the line. You can apply half the tiles, slide them back into position, then let the glue set before moving on to the other side. Work your way around the egg to spread out the weight of the tiles. Add tiles in rows working out to the ends.

6. Let the glue dry for 24 hours.

7. Gently grout the egg with your gloved fingers, working the grout into the small crevices. Remove any excess grout with a damp sponge. Be careful not to knock any tiles loose.

8. Let the grout dry for 20 minutes. Gently remove the grout from the surface of the tiles with a soft towel.

9. Let the grout dry overnight, then buff the tiles again with a soft, clean towel.

119

Materials

Materials
glass votive
clear colored glass, cut into ½-inch tiles
7 teal glass beads
7 blue glass beads
silicone or epoxy glue (can also use Weldbond)
face mask
sanded grout
bucket
sponge
latex gloves

1. To get an idea of how many tiles you'll need for this project, measure the top of the votive with paper or ribbon cut to fit. Lay the tiles out on the paper to determine the design.

2. There is no way to prime glass as you did with the Styrofoam or wooden egg. Sliding tiles may therefore be a challenge. Rest the votive on a folded towel and patiently keep sliding tiles back in place until the glue sets.

3. Apply adhesive to the glass base and allow it to get tacky. Butter the glass bead or tile and apply it. Hold it in place for a few seconds until the glue bonds. When you have attached all the tiles, allow the glue to dry for 24 hours.

4. Mix and apply the grout, taking care not to knock off any tiles. The edges stick out just a bit and are easy to catch with a sponge or towel.

5. Allow the grout to dry for 15 to 20 minutes, then polish the tiles with a soft cloth. After the grout has dried overnight, polish the tiles again.

Materials

table	
sandpaper	
beach glass	
grout	
brushes	
bucket	
palette or craft knife	
squeegee	
sponge	
soft cloth or paper towel or newspaper	
latex gloves	
polyurethane	

1. Sand the tabletop. Arrange the beach glass tiles on the lid to create a design to your liking.

2. Starting in a corner, butter each tile with adhesive and place it on the tabletop. Remember to allow a ⅛-inch gap between the tiles for the grout.

Projects

5. Prepare the grout and apply it, taking care to fill in all the gaps. Remove the excess grout. Let it sit for 15 to 20 minutes, then wipe the tiles with a sponge. After allowing the grout to dry overnight, polish the tiles with a soft cloth.

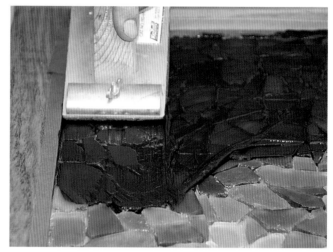

3. You might need to use needle-nose pliers to place the tiny pieces after the larger pieces have been set.

4. Allow the glue to dry overnight, then place masking tape around the wooden rim of the lid to protect it.

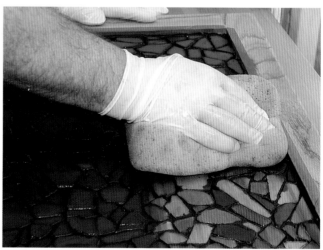

6. To protect the tabletop and enhance the shine of the glass, you can apply several coats of polyurethane.

by Mike Huffman of The Glass Gallery

Materials

terra-cotta saucer or concrete bird bath

layout paper

scissors

permanent marker

contact paper

Epoxy6000, silicone, or cement-based adhesive

sanded cement-based grout with acrylic
   admixture for outdoor use

maple wood stain (optional)

all-weather sealer for brick and concrete

safety goggles

latex gloves

filter mask

mixing bowls and a bucket

sponge

⅛-inch notched trowel

lint-free cloth

Stained glass tiles

175 blue/turquoise tiles
   (½ by ¾–inch rectangle)

175 orange (¾-inch square)

40 light orange (¾-inch square)

Projects

1. Draw the design, or reproduce it to the size you want with a photocopier or tracing paper. If your purchased birdbath is a different size, you'll need to adjust the design as well as the number of tiles.

2. Using a glass scorer and running pliers, cut 175 ½- by ¾–inch rectangles for the background tiles. This shape contrasts with the squares in the main design yet still feels "orderly." In this project, the first row of background tiles outlines the central design, a pattern which is known as *opus tesselatum*. The rest of the background tiles are laid in even rows (*opus regulatum*).

3. Cut 175 bright orange ¾-inch squares for the body and arms of the starfish.

4. Cut 40 light orange ¾-inch squares for the inner body of the starfish.

5. Cut a piece of contact paper several inches larger all around than the mosaic. Remove the backing and lay the paper down with the sticky side facing up. Place the design under the clear contact paper so you can see it.

6. Place orange tiles face down along the outer edges of the starfish, then fill in the arms and the middle of the body.

7. Outline the starfish with the blue rectangle tiles of the background. Starting at the inner V between each arm of the starfish, move up one side and then up the other to create a continuous line of tiles.

8. Next, lay the blue rectangles that run along the outer edge of the circle, linking all the arms of the starfish.

9. Fill in the deep Vs between each arm of the starfish with blue rectangles. Cut to fit as needed.

10. Prepare the base to receive the tiles. You may use Epoxy6000, silicone, or cement-based adhesive for outdoor use. Apply a ⅛-inch layer of adhesive to the inside of the birdbath. If you use a cement-based adhesive, you can use a plastic fork to make grooves in the adhesive that reach down to the base.

11. Pick up the sheet of contact paper with the mosaic on it by the corners. Be careful—it will be heavy. You may need to ask someone to hold the bottom of the sheet by the corners and help you turn the entire piece over to put it in place.

12. Position the outer edge of the design on the top edge of the birdbath, then gently lower the center of the design into the birdbath. When you have placed the center of the design into the adhesive, work your way up the sides of the bowl, continuing to press the tiles into place. No tiles should extend above the top. With fingers spread, gently press each area of the design into the adhesive to be sure that all the tiles are attached.

13. Let the glue dry for 24 hours. Remove the contact paper by pulling it loose at four or five places around the top edge. Gently peel back sections of the paper, keeping one hand on the tiles beneath, to prevent pulling any loose. If a tile does come loose, scrape the old adhesive off the back of the tile and the base. Apply a new layer of glue to the base and the tile. Let it dry before grouting.

14. To get very smooth grout, you can sift the grout powder through a window screen to remove the larger pieces of sand. If you choose to do this, wear a face mask and sift the grout outside. Using the latex admixture for weatherproofing, mix the grout to a fairly stiff, peanut-butter–like consistency.

15. Apply grout with your gloved hands to each area of the mosaic. Use a circular motion to work the grout into the crevices between the tiles. Wipe any excess grout off the face of the tiles.

16. When the grout has dried to a powdery finish (15 to 20 minutes), use a damp sponge to clean the tiles. Rinse the sponge after each wipe to remove any sand. Keep wiping the tiles until all traces of the grout are gone. Let it dry for several hours, then polish the tiles with a cloth.

17. Optional step: Outdoor grout takes two to four days to dry. Once dry, this birdbath and grout were stained with maple wood stain to achieve a light brown color. To do this, wipe the stain on with a cloth, allow it to sit for 15 to 20 minutes, then wipe it off. If you are content with gray grout and concrete, you don't need the wood stain.

18. To protect your birdbath from the extremes of weather, apply an all-purpose sealer. Rub it on the cement and the mosaic with a rag and let it set for 20 minutes. Wipe off any excess sealer with a paper towel. Apply two coats and let cure for 24 hours. The goal is to make your project waterproof so no water gets under the grout and breaks the tiles. You may want to protect the birdbath with a tarp over the winter or bring it inside the garage or basement.

Projects

125

Additional Designs

Teapot

Heart

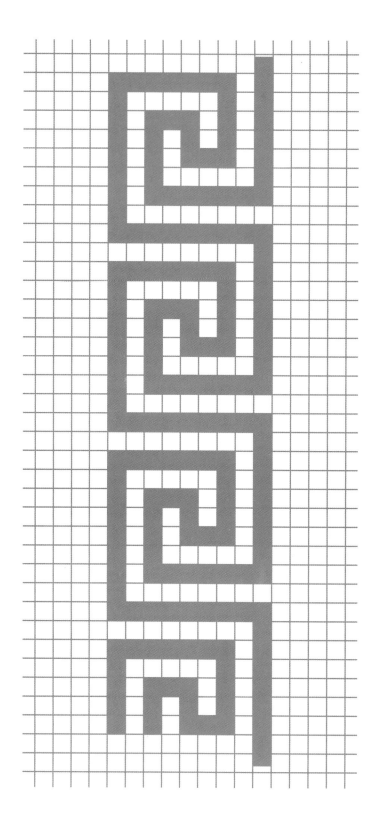

Greek Key

Resources

BOOKS

Ebeling, Eric. *Basic Stained Glass Making.* Mechanics-burg, PA: Stackpole Books, 2003.

Hunkin, Tessa. *Modern Mosaic: Inspiration from the 20th Century.* London: Firefly Books, 2003.

Mills, Teresa. *The Mosaic Artist's Bible: 300 Traditional and Contemporary Designs.* North Pomfret, VT: Trafalgar Square Books, 2005.

Skye, Laurel. *Mosaic Renaissance: Millefiori in Mosaics.* Iola, WI: North Light Books, 2009.

SUPPLIERS AND ARTISTS

Artful Crafter
www.artfulcrafter.com
Sells mosaic tiles, supplies, and stained glass.

Carreaux de Ceramique
Le village - 30140 Atuech
Tel: 04.66.61.83.96
www.ceramique-decoration.com
Handmade tiles and mosaic tables, bathrooms, furniture, house number signs, and more.

Classical Mosaics
www.classicalmosaics.com
Website includes mosaic-making demonstrations as well as photographs of ancient mosaic designs.

The Glass Gallery
1215 George Washington Highway
Yorktown, VA 23693
757-873-3983
www.theglassgallery.biz
Teaches mosaic and stained glass classes and sells tiles and supplies.

Jill Rowland
www.mosaicsbyjill.com
Mirrors, pictures, and gifts for dog owners.

Laurel Skye
http://homepage.mac.com/laurelskye
Teaches workshops and sells tiles and supplies.

Monster Mosaics
www.monstermosaics.com
Sells supplies and has mosaic gallery for inspiration.

Mosaic Mercantile
www.mosaicmercantile.com
Online resource for quality mosaic tile, tools, kits, and accessories.

Mosaic Tools
www.mosaictools.com
Sells a wide variety of tiles, tools, and other materials.

Society of American Mosaic Artists (SAMA)
www.americanmosaics.org
Membership includes a quarterly newsletter, exhibition opportunities, inclusion in an online gallery, a members' directory, and more for the professional mosaic artist.

Stackpole Basics

All the Skills and Tools You Need to Get Started

- Straightforward, expert instruction on a variety of crafts, hobbies, and sports
- Step-by-step, easy-to-follow format
- Current information on equipment and prices for the beginner
- Full-color photography and illustrations
- Convenient lay-flat spiral binding

BASIC STAINED GLASS MAKING
$19.95, 144 pages, 754 color photos,
24 illustrations, 0-8117-2846-3

BASIC KNITTING
$19.95, 108 pages, 377 color photos,
50 color illustrations, 0-8117-3178-2

BASIC CANDLE MAKING
$19.95, 104 pages, 600 color photos,
0-8117-2476-X

BASIC DRIED FLOWER ARRANGING
$16.95, 96 pages, 234 color photos,
0-8117-2863-3

BASIC QUILTING
$19.95, 128 pages, 437 color photos,
11 illustrations, 0-8117-3348-3

BASIC PICTURE FRAMING
$19.95, 108 pages, 374 color photos,
0-8117-3109-X

BASIC JEWELRY MAKING
$19.95, 116 pages, 490 color photos,
12 illustrations, 0-8117-3263-0

BASIC CROCHETING
$19.95, 120 pages, 219 color photos,
27 illustrations, 0-8117-3316-5

Available at your favorite retailer,
or from Stackpole Books at (800) 732-3669

STACKPOLE BOOKS

www.stackpolebooks.com